ERIN COUPE

I CAN FIT THAT IN

HOW ~~ROUTINES~~ *RITUALS*
TRANSFORM YOUR LIFE

Erin Coupe
I Can Fit That In

Copyright © 2025 by H2Lsquared Media
First Edition

Softcover ISBN 979-8-9986081-0-0
Hardcover ISBN 979-8-9986081-1-7
eBook ISBN 979-8-9986081-3-1
Audiobook ISBN 979-8-9986081-2-4

All rights reserved under International and Pan-American Copyright Conventions.

Manufactured in Canada.

For information about discounts for bulk purchases, contact **info@erincoupe.com**

No part of this publication may be reproduced, stored in, or introduced into a retrieval system, transmitted in any form or by any means (electronic, mechanical, photocopying, recording, or otherwise), and/or otherwise used in any manner for purposes of training artificial intelligence technologies to generate text, including, without limitation, technologies that are capable of generating works in the same style or genre as this publication, without the prior written permission of the publisher.

This book is sold subject to the condition that it shall not, by way of trade or otherwise, be lent, resold, hired out, or otherwise circulated without the publisher's prior written consent in any form of binding, cover, or condition other than that in which it was published.

Book Cover Design | Lou Dahl
Book Interior Design | Petya Tsankova
Creative Director | Brooke Adams
Editor | Justin Chevrier
Publishing Management | TSPA The Self Publishing Agency, Inc.

Praise for the Author and *I Can Fit That In*

"Erin has a remarkable way of making time feel expansive, as if anything is truly possible. We've partnered across various organizations, and her authenticity, presence, and unwavering commitment to living fully have profoundly transformed how people lead and engage with life. I bring Erin into teams because her impact is lasting, meaningful, and deeply real. She consistently brings presence, clarity, and emotional depth into every space she enters."

Olga Spivak, Chief Human Resources Officer, WealthTech and Private Equity

"Erin's insights and approach came into my life just as I was taking on the weight of my first CEO role. She helped me find clarity, resilience, and—perhaps most importantly—a more sustainable, healthier way to lead and live. Her wisdom is a blueprint for anyone who wants success without sacrificing well-being."

RJ Hilgers, Two-Time CEO and Career Executive in Advertising, Marketing, and Digital Innovation

"*I Can Fit That In* has profoundly shaped how I approach leadership development within our organization. Erin's thoughtful and compelling framework has helped me empower our leaders to trade burnout and overwhelm for intentionality and clarity. This book is a powerful tool that helps high-performing executives lead not just effectively, but sustainably—across all areas of work and life—rooted in what truly matters."

Carmen Smith, Chief Human Resources Officer of Fortune 1000 Companies

"With wisdom and compassion, Erin Coupe offers a profound roadmap for anyone who is tired—tired of struggling, of being an overachiever, of always being stressed out. In actionable steps, she leads us to a new way of being that is completely in alignment with the qualities we value the most and for that, we are very lucky to have this book in the world."

Lodro Rinzler, Author of *The Buddha Walks into a Bar* ... and *Take Back Your Mind*

"*I Can Fit That In* is an essential guide for the modern executive who's ready to redefine success with more humanity, well-being, and soul. Erin's Ritual Loop Framework is a profound yet practical pathway to transformation from the inside out—in life and leadership. I want to live in a world where this intentional approach is the expectation, not the exception."

Shelley Paxton, Former CMO of Harley-Davidson, now Chief Soul Officer, Keynote Speaker, and Bestselling Author of *Soulbbatical*

"Erin's session had the most registrants out of any we offered—and wow, that was amazing! Over 2,700 emojis came through the screen during your virtual session. People were highly engaged."

VP, Learning and Development, Global Pharmaceutical Company

"Erin's keynote was extraordinary—engaging, authentic, and filled with insights that resonated across our entire International Women's Day event. Her engaging presence captured the hearts and minds of everyone in the audience."

Women's ERG Committee, Global Medical-Surgical Products and Supply Chain Solutions

"Erin reminded us that we are human first. Her keynote was exactly what our top 200 leaders needed: inspiring, authentic, and packed with actionable insights."

Chief People Officer, Global Container Shipping and Supply Chain Management

"I can't recommend Erin enough—we have all walked away better leaders and better people because of her and this program!"

VP of People, e-Commerce Technology Firm

"Working with Erin is a partnership in every sense of the word. The impact of her work was profound. She elevated the experience for everyone present."

Program Manager, Law Firm eDiscovery

"Erin's work is transformative, and our leaders walked away with a tangible toolkit they could reference as they practiced her teachings."

VP of Human Capital, Engineering and Technology Company

"Erin empowers us by creating a space where our voices are not just heard but celebrated ... reminding us to pause, reflect, and prioritize our well-being. She left us with a sense of unity and resilience."

Director, Women in eDiscovery

"I'm a dedicated journaler and to compare my mindset pre- and post-Erin are night and day. She's truly made my life (and my family's life) much better. It almost feels like I have a mini superpower!"

CFO, Technology Company

"Erin helped me find my center and return to my path. Whether you're struggling to find meaning or simply looking to improve your experience on earth, work with Erin. Living your best life may depend on it."

Founder and Chief Executive, Technology Company

"Erin's inspirational personal story, her key messages on overcoming adversity, her focus on self-care in order to be better for others as leaders … truly resonated."

Chief People Officer, Global Fortune 350 Company

"Erin is an amazing speaker. I probably could have used some of her techniques before my presentation that morning lol, but now I have new tools going forward."

Senior Manager, Top Tax and Accounting Firm

"Thank you, Erin, for sharing your light with the team. Humanity exists to discover its humanity. Which is what you authentically guided us to do."

Chief Executive, Professional Sports Organization

"Let the heart drive success! I'm glad to have gone through this training and I thank professionals like Erin for exposing self-awareness."

Senior Executive, Engineering and Manufacturing

"Even after practicing mindfulness for years, I hadn't spent much time considering how valuable this practice can be in our professional lives. Thank you Erin!"

Senior Executive, Top Global Consulting Firm

"Erin met our leaders where they were and created a space of reflection, authenticity, and growth. This was the absolute best way to start out our Director Summit for our attendees and we're excited to be able to weave the learnings and takeaways into the remainder of the sessions."

Senior Director, Freight Transportation and Logistics

"Erin's teachings don't just change how you lead—they change how you live."

Executive, Finance and Wealth Management

"I once again learned a lot from Erin; she gave me a lot to think about as a leader, parent, spouse, and person."

CEO, WealthTech and FinTech Industry

"The power to start a chain reaction of compassion and support ... That is what Erin gives her clients."

Executive Leader, Global Furniture Manufacturing

"Erin provided tangible tools and a lasting sense of empowerment—our team is already applying what we learned."

Partner, Law Firm Private Equity Practice Leader

"Erin gave us permission to pause—and that small shift has made a big impact on how I lead."

Leader, Fortune 200 Commercial Real Estate Firm

"Erin meets you with deep empathy and practical wisdom—her work opened a new path forward for me."

Leader, Global Furniture Manufacturing

Dedication

For Craig—
My partner in life, in love, in friendship, and in soul evolution.

You've seen every version of me. You've held space through the unraveling and cheered me on through the becoming. Thank you for your unwavering support, belief in me (even when I doubted myself), and the room you've given me to expand into who I truly am—these pages would not exist without you.

Thank you for walking beside me in the truest way. For traveling this world with me through airports and countrysides, oceans and trails, city streets and quiet corners. For savoring conversations with strangers who become friends, living like locals wherever we go, and pausing in reverence for the beauty of this earth—from glowing sunrises to the flowers, birds, and bunnies in our own backyard. For sharing a love of culture, of people, and of seeking more from life, not through accumulation, but through depth.

You remind me, daily, that what matters most isn't what we accomplish, but how fully we live. You are my greatest encourager, my steady ground, and my forever soulmate.

$H2L^2$
Our symbol for the life we're consciously creating since day one: honest, expansive, rooted in love, and always reaching toward the next soulful horizon.

Table of Contents

Hi, I'm Erin.   1

INTRODUCTION
    The Question That Changed Everything   3
    The Power of *I Can Fit That In*   19

PART 1: ACTIVATING SELF-AWARENESS
    Chapter 1: Awakening from Autopilot   33
    Chapter 2: Challenging Outdated Beliefs   47
    Chapter 3: Rewiring Your Mindset   63
    Chapter 4: Reigniting Your Inner Spark   81

PART 2: TRANSFORMING YOUR LIFE THROUGH RITUALS
    Chapter 5: Harnessing the Power of Rituals   97
    Chapter 6: Building a Sustainable Life   115
    Chapter 7: Protecting Your Peace   133
    Chapter 8: Navigating Resistance with Grace and Grit   149

PART 3: LIVING WITH CLARITY, INTENTION, AND IMPACT
    Chapter 9: Sustaining a Life That Fuels You   173
    Chapter 10: Externalizing Empowerment   185

CONCLUSION
    The Life You Were Meant to Lead   193

APPENDIX
    A Living Reminder: You Can Fit That In   205
    Acknowledgements   207
    Bibliography   211
    About Erin   215
    Share the Love   217
    Book Erin to Speak at Your Next Event   219
    Stay in Touch with Me   221

Hi, I'm Erin.

I wrote this book because I felt trapped in a life that looked successful on the outside but, on the inside, was hollow and disconnected. For years, I chased the illusion of control through rigid routines, hyper-productivity, and overcommitment, believing that if I just did more, I could quiet the chaos within. But the truth I eventually uncovered and the one I want to share with you is this: Doing more will never cure the emptiness you feel inside.

The mindset you develop as a child and inherit as an adult—the unquestioned beliefs you hold, the deeply rooted and ignored emotions, the patterns you cling to—continues to pilot your life long after the events that formed it took place.

This book is my invitation to you to take back control of your mindset: to step off the hamster wheel, to break free from the mindlessness that you've accepted with the misguided hope that "someday" you'll be happy, and to move toward an intentional, soul-aligned way of leading your life.

You are not fundamentally broken and doomed to remain feeling stuck. If you're reading this right now, you already possess the drive you need to transform your life of reaction and autopilot routines into a meaning-infused ritual-based life that is deeply fulfilling, clear, and energizing.

I Can Fit That In is not just a mindset shift—it's a life preserver for those who have become numb to the chaos around and within them. If you're willing to put in the hard work to hold on and radically change your life, you will find yourself on firm ground—potentially for the first time in your life—with the tools you need to reclaim your life, your time, and your power.

INTRODUCTION

The Question That Changed Everything

It was a Friday night in August 2017. I had just poured a glass of cabernet, sank into the couch next to my husband Craig, and without warning, the words tumbled out of me:

Why do we do this to ourselves? What's the meaning of any of it?

I didn't realize it then, but that moment would mark the beginning of everything changing—from the inside out.

Up to that point, my life had been a masterclass in keeping everything together. I held an executive position, spent ten hours a week commuting, managed my kids' needs and schedules, maintained a spotless house and the never-ending projects of home ownership, and plowed through strenuous workouts that matched the intensity of my overloaded nervous system. I'd be remiss if I didn't mention the daily five-thirty glass of wine that "took the edge off."

Every day felt like *Groundhog Day*—relentless, dutiful, numbing. I had ignored it for years, spending far too much energy and time looking everywhere outside myself for the answer: the next promotion, the new company, a higher salary, a bigger title, better vacations. I was never satisfied, always chasing something just out of reach—trying to rearrange the external world to make my inner world feel better. Or perhaps by constantly seeking something else, I was unconsciously distracting myself from the truth I needed to face: I wasn't living *my* life and I wasn't happy living someone else's either.

What I hadn't yet realized was how I had trained myself to think about efficiency and effectiveness through the lens of other people's expectations. And in doing so, I deprioritized myself. Like a fisherman tossing scraps back into the ocean, I was throwing away what truly mattered to me—my time, my energy, my focus—and feeding it to the endless routines and obligations I believed I had to maintain.

But that Friday night, something shifted. The voice grew too loud to ignore. For the first time, I allowed the question to come forward—and for the first time, I truly listened. Not to the world's demands, but to my own heart.

My Story: From Surviving Life to Self-Leadership

In our high-functioning, fast-moving world, it's easy to ignore the internal nudges that ask you to consider how you're living your life. That is, until something cracks you open.

For me, that crack started long before I could articulate it.

When I was five years old, my forty-five-year-old father woke up one morning paralyzed from the waist down. There had been no warning, no time to prepare. I watched, frozen, as he was carried out of our home. The life he had once known was slipping away before my eyes.

My family's world changed for the worse overnight as everything came crashing down. Dad was in the Veterans hospital (a resource thanks to his brief service in the air force as a teenager) for months, diagnosed first with Guillain–Barré syndrome, a rare neurological disorder where the body's immune system attacks the nervous system. Then, the double whammy of a diagnosis with the highest severity of lupus, a chronic autoimmune disease where the body's immune system attacks its own tissues, permanently damaging the organs and systems.

As fast as the summer always seems to fly by, his beautifully olive-toned skin permanently turned splotchy pink and white. Oxygen tanks replaced his breath, and he aged so rapidly that kids at school often asked if my grandfather was picking me up. The quiet shame I carried deepened as I grew older.

My childhood became a blur of hospital stays, prescription pill sorters (he swallowed no fewer than thirty pills a day just to sustain a painfully diminished quality of life), caretaking in more ways than one, silent prayers, and constant, heavy vigilance.

To say I grew up fast would be an understatement. I was catapulted through my adolescence.

Up until that point, we were a working-class, blue-collar family doing just fine. My mother, the eldest of six, had started nursing school at eighteen but was forced to quit just a year later to take a job in retail and help support her struggling parents. She never realized her dream of having a nursing career. My father had worked in protective services as a security guard, but when he became terminally ill, the burden of supporting us fell entirely on my mother's shoulders. The financial strain was overwhelming. We slipped below the poverty line, and the muffled day-to-day struggle of making ends meet became our new normal.

Mom was thrust into raising three children with no roadmap and only a fraction of the life partner she once had—who she also now had to care for. She did everything she could just to keep us afloat. We lost our home and lived in motels where my mom worked as a maid and as a waitress at the Waffle House across the street. It helped to have both jobs, as gas money was a luxury we could barely afford. I remember going to work with her many times. Looking back, there's something almost endearing about how the five-to-six-year-old me developed an appetite for extra crispy, extra cheesy hashbrowns—and I even learned how to make a tight bed. I'm sure Admiral William H. McRaven, author of *Make Your Bed*, would've given me an A+.

There were small glimmers of light and hope back then. Coloring in the back of the donut shop where my mom once worked—gosh, it smelled so good. Watching her drive the school bus for my class field trips—the innocence of childhood made me think that was the coolest thing. Making jewelry with my aunt and grandma, then helping to sell it at craft fairs. These moments were tiny pockets of light, but they couldn't outweigh the prevailing energy of imbalance and entropy. The collective mentality of my family remained the same: Just get by. Just survive.

Then came a moment I'll never forget. When I was eighteen years old and a sophomore in college, I was pulled out of my economics class and given a Post-it with a number to call. After a panicked walk to the campus office, I dialed the number.

> "Hello?" said a voice I didn't recognize.
> "Hi, this is Erin. I got a message to call this number."
> "Hold on, honey, I'll get your mom."

And as the phone was passed to her, the dreadfulness was passed to me.

> "Erin, Dad died this morning," Mom said, sobbing.

The weight of the unexpected news buckled my knees, and the room went black.

Later that morning, lying next to his cold, lifeless body in the hospital room, I was consumed not only by grief, but by a strange, urgent curiosity—an ache from within as I tried to understand the incomprehensible loss.

> *What does it really mean to be alive?*
> *What is the meaning of life, truly, beyond survival?*
> *What are we when everything we know disappears?*

These questions didn't feel philosophical or out of place in that moment. They felt essential—basic. Little did I know that they were the foundation of a better future—one where I wasn't just surviving, but truly living.

My father's life—and his death—planted something inside me: a quiet, unshakable confidence that I knew what was at stake. I felt a deep longing to not just endure, but to experience life fully.

Though I couldn't articulate it then, I made a silent vow to myself: I will not live only to survive. I will find a way to thrive. I will build a life that is wholly my own.

But knowing and doing are two very different things—especially when you're on your own, with no clear direction and no one to help you find the way forward.

The Part I Never Thought I'd Share

As I started writing this book, I knew there was a part of my story that I didn't want to share. A part so deeply hidden that for years, I let it stay buried beneath the surface, hoping it would fade. But if I'm going to ask you to be real about the experiences that have formed your mindset—the moments that are more easily numbed away rather than dealt with in a healthy manner—I owe it to you to honor mine.

During those years of survival after my father got sick, money was so tight that my mother eventually resorted to survival tactics that some may not agree with. There were times I recall going into the gas station to pay for just three dollars of gas, paying with rolls of pennies that we'd scrounged together. Our utilities were turned off more times than I can count. My parents would argue late into the night about who they could borrow money from next to pay overdue bills and the mounting late fees. But there were times when there wasn't anyone to borrow from. And so, my mother sometimes resorted to writing checks that she knew wouldn't clear.

She didn't do it out of malice or recklessness, but out of desperation. It was the only way to put shoes on our feet, stave off another utility shut-off notice, and pay the rent. Sometimes, it worked. Sometimes, it didn't. And when those checks bounced, the consequences weren't small or easy to fix; they were heavy, casting shadows over our family that lingered far longer than the current moment of crisis.

From the time I was seven, I saw police cars pull up at our home, in store parking lots, and on the side of the highway more times than any child should. It was as if she were being hunted for a crime she didn't commit. Flashing lights. Handcuffs. Uniformed officers taking my mother away. I remember screaming for her, pleading with them not to do this. I shrank down, holding my breath, watching her be led out like a criminal—all for trying to hold our fragile world together. I remember thinking: *When will I see her again? What will people at school think? What do I say when she's just ... gone? How do I survive without her?*

Collect calls from correctional centers were almost always on the other end of the line (or bill collectors). We wrote letters by hand to judges and parole officers, petitioning for understanding: *She's not a bad person. She just did what she had to so we didn't end up on the street.*

This cycle repeated off and on for more than a decade. There were long stretches when her voice on the other end of a jail phone and the pages-long letters she'd send were the only things anchoring me. And as I got older and the innocence of childhood faded away, there were the visits I dreaded—my sisters and I stepping into those dreary, stark correctional facilities that Mom had been forced to call home for months and years on end. Seeing her that way was deeply sad. The last time she was taken away was my junior year of college. She missed a lot over the years, including my college graduation.

The weight of that trauma lingered long after the last time she was released. It lodged itself in my nervous system, crystalizing into the belief that I had a secret to hide and that I had to outrun the shame. It buried fear deep inside me—a fear that if I ever stopped chasing and doing more, everything would collapse and I would face the same fate as my mother. Even after I graduated college, the scarcity mindset instilled in me by my mother's situation had marred the clarity of mind I had when I said goodbye to my father, and living out that contradiction would keep me bound for decades.

The Cost of Living Someone Else's Life

Like so many—though perhaps with an even deeper desire to break free from what I was born into—I set out to create a better life in the only way I thought I knew how: by chasing the version of success that society told me equated to happiness.

I put myself through college—the first generation in my family to earn a four-year degree—with the help of grants, work-study jobs, student loans, and academic scholarships. If there was a will, there was a way. I graduated magna cum laude, landed my first professional role in client service at Reuters, and by the time I was twenty-four, moved to New York City without knowing a single soul. Shortly after, I was recruited as a business analyst at Goldman Sachs.

On paper, it was everything I thought I wanted: prestige, security, accomplishment.

But, inside, a different story was unfolding.

My body became my first messenger. Intense migraines, mysterious rashes, fainting spells, debilitating anxiety attacks—my nervous system was speaking the truth my mind refused to hear. I was still living in survival mode—only now I was dressed in more expensive clothes and dined at real restaurants instead of fast food chains.

Working at Goldman Sachs became an exhausting battle—a relentless grind against a culture that prized micromanagement over humanity. For years, I reported to women that resented me due to their own insecurities. I was a hard worker who wanted to be liked and rewarded for my efforts. I fought to meet impossible expectations, to outpace exhaustion, to silence the quiet panic rising in my chest. I traded intuition for achievement, well-being for validation. I kept pushing, numbing, achieving—*that's just what you do, right?* The little girl inside me was convinced that's how you "make it."

My well-being suffered not solely because of external pressures, but because I hadn't yet cultivated the mindset and human skills to manage my time, focus, and energy. I didn't yet know how to protect my peace, to honor my boundaries, or to lead with peace from within.

Over time as I stepped into more senior leadership roles in Fortune 150 companies, the pace accelerated. The titles became bigger, the responsibilities grew heavier. But it wasn't the companies or the increased demands of leadership that broke me. It was, yet again, the way I approached it all: everything and everyone at the expense of myself. I was chasing perfection, craving more, always looking to the next benchmark. Contentment felt like a betrayal of ambition; gratitude felt like complacency.

And then came the reckoning. After getting married to Craig, having children, and moving to suburban Chicago, I found myself one evening standing in the center of the so-called perfect life I had built—the house, the money, the accolades, the social calendar—and realizing I was totally numb and felt utterly hollow.

The professional success I had fought so hard to achieve felt startlingly empty. Each day became a race against chronic exhaustion. The life I was chasing wasn't mine—I had inherited someone else's version of success—and living that life left me feeling numb. I had managed to avoid some of the worst fears that my mother's life had taught me, but in the process, I completely forgot about the promises I made to myself at my father's bedside.

A Leap of Faith (and Fear)

Six months after that initial discussion with Craig, in the midst of my numbness, a strange and wild opportunity presented itself: a leadership retreat in Bali.

Twelve women, a week of self-development, oceans away from my responsibilities. I entered the two-for-the-price-of-one giveaway on social media almost absentmindedly, convinced it wasn't meant for someone like me—a mother, a wife, a corporate leader with many obligations. My mind told me it was for yogis, entrepreneurs, or people who were further along in their lives.

But my soul had other plans. I won the giveaway. And the universe, in its wonderfully poetic way, gave me a sign: the chandelier above our bed flickered harmoniously the moment I heard the news. It had never flickered before. It never flickered since. Craig as my witness.

Still, the guilt was deafening. *Could I really leave? Was I selfish? Was I irresponsible?* But beneath the noise of fear, a deeper voice whispered:

> *This is for you. Say yes to yourself.*

The fear didn't vanish just because I said yes. Three hours into the flight to Bali, I fainted in the airplane restroom—a literal collapse under the weight of decades of overextension and self-abandonment. A metaphorical reset.

When I arrived at the retreat, I was depleted, disoriented, and secretly terrified. One of our first assignments was deceptively simple: Record a video answering, *"Who am I?"* I realized I had no idea.

I had built my entire existence around external achievement, but stripped of titles, accolades, and roles, I didn't know how to answer the question. What surfaced initially was raw and painful, as I came up with a few answers:

A prover	A self-saboteur
A planner	A people-pleaser
A performer	A trauma survivor

A life constructed on survival strategies and coping mechanisms.

It was in that discomfort—the recognition that I had identified myself with titles my whole adult life and didn't truly know who I really was underneath them—that I finally glimpsed the truth: I am not here to live anyone else's life or by their version of success. I am here to live a life anchored in my authentic identity and fueled by a calm, confident presence that is connected to my soul. At least, that's the yearning I'd been sensing deep down long before this trip.

I am here to live a life anchored in my authentic identity and fueled by a calm, confident presence that is connected to my soul.

And I began to realize that I wasn't alone.

In deeper, refreshingly honest conversations with other leaders and high achievers after the retreat, some common threads emerged:

- We had traded our self-confidence for approval.
- We had followed the scripts we were handed, rarely questioning whether they reflected our values or would ever lead to personal fulfillment.
- We had achieved financial and professional success, but in the process, we had abandoned ourselves.

Achievement without alignment had become the silent epidemic no one in the professional world was talking about. And I was living proof.

But here's what I also knew, with unwavering clarity: It wasn't too late to choose differently. I was done waiting for life to change. I was ready to reclaim my life.

Rebuilding My Life from the Inside Out

For me, awakening didn't arrive like a lightning strike on the Bali trip, and reclaiming my life was not a quick process. It evolved slowly, in countless tiny defiant acts of presence and grounding amidst the relentless current of the world around me.

It wasn't easy. For so long, I was entangled in anxiousness. I had the gnawing sense that there was never enough time for me, and a deeper fear that I would never quite get to where I truly wanted to go because I was too busy managing everything else. That level of micro-worrying consumed my energy and attention, leaving me depleted and disconnected from what actually mattered.

Piece by piece, I started to release that grip. I turned inward, empowered by self-awareness practices and rituals that rooted me in the present—as simple as a deep breath, a morning coffee savored in stillness, or reclaiming a few moments of quiet reflection.

I began to notice subtle signs from the universe that I was onto something: the ladybugs kept showing up (my father's favorite), cardinals claimed my yard as their territory, or the genuinely real and personal conversation with someone I'd just met. I started to hear a deeper truth: Survival is not the same as living. Fulfillment isn't a destination, it's a daily choice to return to yourself.

Survival is not the same as living.

As I practiced inner work and ritualized my well-being, my external life slowly transformed. Moments of frantic busyness gave way to intentional rhythms. Autopilot gave way to mindfulness. Scarcity thinking gave way to gratitude.

My relationship with motherhood shifted as well. What I once viewed as a burden or obligation became a source of laughter, tenderness, and deeper connection. My marriage began to flourish as I softened with vulnerability, shared my feelings more openly, relaxed where I used to get rigid, and listened more intently.

Craig noticed these changes in me long before I fully recognized them in myself. I'll never forget him telling me, "Honey, you're more calm and patient when usually you wouldn't be." Words I never thought I'd hear. I guess the proof really is in the pudding.

From Personal Alignment to Professional Empowerment

The inner transformation didn't stay confined to my personal life; it spilled into how I led and lived professionally. The rituals that helped me reclaim my energy and presence personally and at home soon began to transform how I showed up at work.

Through the rituals I introduced and embraced—those simple, consistent acts of presence and self-honoring—I began to nurture a different way to lead. I began to soften the grip of control and shift from force to flow. I let go of the need to know everything and started showing up more honest and transparent. I was becoming more whole and it empowered others to be better and do better.

I began leading with compassion, relinquishing control while slowing down to mentor and support others. I modeled self-care not as a weakness, but as a strength. The more I grounded myself, the more I shared my ideas, spoke up where I used to stay silent, and let people get closer to the real me. I started to embody authenticity—something that had felt virtually impossible in my past.

I learned that my nervous system—the very core of my presence—set the tone for every room I entered. Where I once only noticed the energy in a room or the chemistry between my team and a prospective client, I now recognized the role my own presence played in creating that energy. Through personal rituals, I brought steadiness to chaos, clarity to complexity, and calm to tense moments. I modeled a new kind of leadership—one rooted in authenticity, resilience, and humanity.

The impact was undeniable. As I became more grounded and authentic in my leadership (not just checking boxes to drive results), I noticed something profound: I began attracting dream clients and opportunities bigger than anything I had encountered before. My relationships and reputation in the industry flourished. I was no longer chasing clients, they were coming to me. People wanted to know me more, to work with me, to be around the energy I radiated. It was as if I had become a beacon of light, and like moths to a flame, people were naturally drawn in.

The shifts didn't go unnoticed. I was approached by upper management to help the broader organizational culture—to make it a healthier, more collaborative place to work. This wasn't just about me leading differently; it was about catalyzing transformation at scale.

The Power of *I Can Fit That In*

> Yesterday I was clever, so I wanted to change the world.
> Today I am wise, so I am changing myself.
>
> Rumi

You've picked up this book because somewhere deep inside, there's a soft nudge, a tug, a whisper—or perhaps by now, a scream—that life must offer more than an endless cycle of meaningless demands, obligations, and busyness. You've achieved success by almost every external measure you've been told to value: impressive job titles, financial stability, and social status. Yet, you can't shake the subtle but pervasive feeling of disconnection, of missing something essential and deeply personal. You long for a meaningful shift—a deep, fundamental realignment of your life around what genuinely nourishes and fulfills you.

This book will guide you toward that shift, not by adding more tasks to your endless to-do list, and not through easy systems or quick hacks to be able to walk around the office with the seeming confidence of a global CEO—instead, this book will guide you to do the hard work to reconnect with your soul and build a deliberate relationship with yourself.

I Can Fit That In is not a time management book. Far from it. *I Can Fit That In* is also not just a phrase. It is a reclamation. An invitation to transform your life of mindless routines that deplete you into a life of meaningful rituals that nourish you. To move from default survival to intentional fulfillment. To fit in what truly matters—not by doing more, but by choosing better. Fitting in what fuels you is made possible first by a mindset shift to believing you can design your life.

Throughout these pages, you will find tools, reflections, practices, and messages designed to bring you back to yourself, anytime and anywhere for the rest of your life. At the core of all meaningful change is a simple, profound truth: You already have what you need. You just have to make space for it.

You are not behind. You are right on time. And I'm thrilled to be on this journey with you.

Making Space for the Right Things

You can't fit more into a life already bursting at the seams. But you can fit in what truly matters.

I Can Fit That In isn't just a philosophy, it's a fundamental shift in how you move through the world. It's the blueprint for reclaiming your time, energy, and focus with clarity, purpose, and intention.

> *You can't fit more into a life already bursting at the seams. But you can fit in what truly matters.*

This is about making space for the right things. About designing a rhythm that nourishes you, fuels your purpose, and allows you to flourish without the burnout, the busyness, or the constant sense of "not enough."

Imagine waking up feeling calm and energized, not because you've nailed some prescriptive routine for 300 consecutive days, but because you've crafted a life around what actually fuels you. Picture yourself walking into meetings, family dinners, or moments of solitude fully present, connected, and unapologetically clear. That's the power of intentional living. That's the outcome this book will guide you toward.

This isn't abstract theory. It's practical. Actionable. Real. You'll move from feeling perpetually pulled in a hundred directions to leading your life with clarity and conviction. You'll stop reacting to the relentless pace of the world and start living from the inside out.

The most powerful transformation requires the removal of what was never truly yours: letting go of what took up space within you, not because you intentionally claimed it, but because you inherited it, absorbed it, or believed it was necessary to survive. The process of fitting in what truly matters is also a process of clearing out what no longer fits—old habits, outdated beliefs, draining commitments, and ways of being that no longer serve the life you're meant to lead.

The true power of *I Can Fit That In* lies in its simplicity and sovereignty. Choosing, moment by moment, how you want to live, feel, and lead. Creating results that are not just impressive, but deeply satisfying.

Yes, you're results-driven and that's a beautiful thing. You're meant to set and get after your goals. Just remember: Lasting impact isn't measured by how much you cram into every hour. It's measured by the depth of your presence, the clarity of your choices, and the energy you bring to what matters most.

And here's the secret: These principles aren't just personal; they redefine how you lead. The most impactful leaders aren't just masters of strategy. They're masters of presence. They move through rooms with a calm, magnetic confidence that inspires teams, energizes cultures, and elevates everything around them. This is not reserved for a select few (though, there was a time when it was). It's a skill—a way of being—you can cultivate.

I Can Fit That In is more than a mantra. It's a methodology. It's the framework for creating a life and leadership style that's as nourishing on the inside as it is powerful on the outside.

It all begins with one profound shift:

I Can Fit That In.

Not as a way to fit more in, but as a way to fit in what truly matters.

This is your turning point. From this moment forward, you're not running on empty. You're choosing to live fully awake, aligned, and ready for whatever comes next.

And when you live this way, you don't just change your own life, you ignite transformation in everyone around you.

How This Book Works

Throughout the book, you'll encounter self-awareness practices and realignment rituals that invite you to step into a more premeditated rhythm. Some of these overlap in timeframe and focus. This is intentional. I encourage you to choose those that resonate most with where you are each week. Let the book guide you, but also trust your intuition about what you need in the moment.

This flexibility helps you avoid the trap of "doing it all" and instead focus on meaningful shifts that truly replenish and align you.

To make the most of this journey:

- **Follow the structure if you seek a guided path.** The chapters are designed to build upon one another, leading you from awakening your awareness to designing and embodying rituals that sustain a fulfilled, vibrant life and bringing this work to your family, community, and leadership.
- **Integrate as you go.** Every chapter offers actionable takeaways—not prescriptions, but invitations—to begin living more intentionally. Choose the tools and practices that resonate most each week and design rituals that serve your present, ever-evolving needs.
- **Return whenever you need to.** Growth isn't linear. Let this book be a touchstone you revisit—whether for clarity, a renewed commitment, or a gentle reminder of what truly matters.
- **Honor your pace.** Transformation is not a race. It's an unfolding. Take your time. Let the insights sink beneath the surface. Lasting change arises not from urgency, but from presence.

This is not about reinventing your life overnight. It is about remembering the life you were always meant to live, and learning to live it with courage and intention.

In **part 1**, you'll focus on disentangling from exhaustion and mindless overcommitment. These chapters awaken you to the patterns and beliefs that have kept you stuck, setting the stage for deeper, more purposeful living.

At the end of each chapter in part 1, you'll encounter a section of **self-awareness practices**—simple, profound activities designed to reconnect you with the present, identify the elements of your mindset, and subtract the narratives and thoughts that no longer belong. Rather than skills to master, these are opportunities to slow down and soften old patterns through intentional self-awareness.

In **part 2**, you'll explore **realignment rituals**—predesigned tools and frameworks to introduce rituals into your daily life, redesigning your schedule in congruence with your rediscovered values, purpose, and energy. This section is where the intentional self-awareness practices of part 1 evolve into proactive rituals that fuel your mind and soul to be the best version of yourself.

In **part 3**, you'll see how the personal transformation you've cultivated becomes a beacon for others. This isn't just about self-leadership, as it's just as much about how you lead at home, at work, and in your community. The best leaders in any industry, the ones who inspire trust and spark cultural change, are not just strategists and visionaries. They are present. They embody the alignment, resilience, and authenticity we explore here. Their "best-kept secret" has always been their commitment to rituals and practices that nourish them from the inside out. It's no longer secret society information. It's a new standard of leadership.

The most lasting transformations rarely happen all at once. They expand in small, conscious decisions—a shift in mindset, a reclaimed morning, a courageous no, a deliberate yes.

This is how you begin living more deeply. And the way forward is inward.

Imagine a life where your choices feel expansive rather than burdensome.

Where you lead not only in boardrooms, Zoom meetings, or your household, but in the quiet, respectful way you show up for yourself, for humanity, and for your deeper calling.

No more autopilot. No more days of numbness on the altar of "someday." It's time to be whole and live fully aligned with what matters most.

PART 1

ACTIVATING SELF-AWARENESS

The Compass Within: Rediscovering Self

We cannot change what we are not aware of, and once we are aware, we cannot help but change.

Sheryl Sandberg, *Lean In*

Before we dive into any new system, tool, or strategy, we must begin with the only place that truly matters: within you. The totality of what makes you *you* is not a footnote in the story; it's the foundation.

Achieving self-awareness is hard, but it is not optional for those who wish to resolve their numbness. And there's no shortcut to awakening. That's exactly why so many avoid it.

A Harvard Business Review study *What Self-Awareness Really Is and How to Cultivate It* found that while 95% of people believe they're self-aware, only 10 to 15% actually are. If it were easy, everyone would do it. But ease was never the point—freedom is.

The truth is this: Self-awareness isn't something to fear. It doesn't diminish you—you're not picking yourself apart. It liberates you. It invites you to see yourself more clearly. When you turn inward with intention, you begin to untangle the patterns you didn't choose, disrupt the momentum that no longer serves you, and remember who you are beneath the performance.

Self-awareness is the cornerstone of everything that follows in this book, and in your life. Without it, no ritual (and certainly no routine) can sustain you and no practice can truly nourish you. Without self-awareness, you remain vulnerable to the noise around you—reacting instead of leading, performing instead of living, and eventually wondering why success feels so hollow.

Without self-awareness, you remain vulnerable to the noise around you.

Self-awareness is something you practice, silently, in the periphery of your day-to-day life. There's no medal to earn or badge of honor to display. It's not another credential to add to your LinkedIn profile. It isn't a performance. It's the quiet, radical act of tuning.

For a long time, I tried to bypass it. I devoured self-help books. I stacked my calendar with "self-care." I tried to outrun emptiness with ambition. But no strategy could silence the ache of being disconnected from myself. Real change didn't come from doing more. It came from listening more deeply and intently making space for myself.

True self-awareness does not mean flaw-finding or endless self-analysis. It's about presence and noticing what triggers you, what energizes you, what stories define you—and learning how to accept it all with compassion and curiosity.

When you cultivate this kind of awareness, you reclaim your power. You begin to choose your life instead of defaulting into it. You design rituals that restore you. You set boundaries that honor you. You align your external life with your internal truth.

Self-awareness is devotion. It's a living practice, not a destination. It grows with every conscious breath, every small act of courage, every moment you choose to return to yourself.

This is where transformation begins.

In this first part of the journey, we will confront the subtle forces that have shaped how you experience your days. You will learn how to

- awaken from autopilot,
- replace outdated beliefs with liberating truths,
- shift your inner dialogue from criticism to compassion,
- reignite your spark and visualize your best self.

This isn't a call to abandon ambition or discipline. I'm as organized, ambitious, and disciplined as they come—in fact, now more so than ever. But it all hits differently. It fuels me rather than depletes me.

This is an invitation to infuse your ambition with consciousness, so your life expands not just in accomplishment, but in meaning.

Self-awareness is seeing—clearly and compassionately—where you have fallen asleep to your own life, and choosing, moment by conscious moment, to awaken.

CHAPTER 1

Awakening from Autopilot

Until you make the unconscious conscious, it will direct your life and you will call it fate.

Carl Jung

I'm not going to tell you to abandon everything in your life in pursuit of a dramatic reinvention. Rather, the first step to conscious living requires the simple but painful effort of allowing yourself to feel where you have previously gone numb. The autopilot system that you've developed over the years has kept you alive, but now is the time to retake your agency. Choice is the seed of change, and you need to prepare the fertile ground of awareness if it's going to take root.

When you practice self-awareness, you realize that you've subconsciously built a number of systems that have kept you sleepwalking: the meetings that pay the bills but drain you, the habits that keep you happy for an evening but ultimately numb you, the markers of success that you can show off but feel hollow because they were never really yours.

Success without presence is empty. And ambition without alignment is just another way of abandoning yourself.

Success without presence is empty.

Routines, at their core, are neither good nor bad. Put simply, they are systems—rhythms the brain uses to conserve energy, to create predictability, to survive. The ego clings to routine because it craves control. Predictability can seem safe, but it can also silently shrink your life. Left unchecked, routines become fortresses that keep out wonder and new possibilities. And in the blur of busyness, the miracle of being alive slips quietly beneath the surface. You didn't consciously choose to live this way. But somewhere along the line, you stopped choosing at all.

In this chapter, you will be invited to fight back against the numbness you've developed through the autopilot routines that you've learned to trust. Those moments of awakening—the ones where you feel like you've finally woken up in your own life—aren't moments of crisis. They are the result of you allowing yourself to inhabit the present.

The Antidote to Mindless Living

You cannot change what you are unwilling to notice.

Mindless living is one of the most seductive traps of modern life. What begins as an efficient way to unwind after a long day can harden into an autopilot routine—an existence not consciously chosen, but simply maintained. Days blur into weeks, weeks into years, and somewhere along the way, the pulse of genuine living fades beneath the noise of doing. Life becomes surface level.

The antidote is awareness. Awakening from autopilot is a continual reclaiming, not a one-time epiphany. It's remembering, moment by moment, that you have the power to choose: To pause. To notice. To pivot.

Awareness interrupts mindlessness. It invites you to consciously participate.

Throughout history, much has been written about the power of habit and the necessity of routine. Entire bookshelves are filled with teachings that champion discipline, repetition, and structured action. And for good reason: Habits can indeed be stabilizing and essential for survival in a complex world.

What I'm offering here may feel, at first, like a contradiction to much of what you've been taught. You've been told to develop your mornings into routines, systematize your productivity, and discipline yourself into excellence. And there is nothing wrong with that approach if it has nourished you. Oftentimes, however, routines become rigid, draining, mindless actions that we just do because we think we have to. The meaning is siphoned out of them over time, even when that's not how they began.

Awareness without action is just another form of delay. It's not enough to notice when old patterns no longer serve you; you must also be willing to challenge them. This is the crossroads where many turn back, choosing the familiarity of exhaustion over the vulnerability of change. Discomfort, ironically, can feel like home simply because it's familiar.

But if you have the courage to lean into that discomfort, to question what you once accepted as truth, then you open the door to a radically different way of living: not faster, not busier, not more forceful—but truer.

This is where agency lives. And agency is where true freedom begins.

Rituals—not routines—become the scaffolding for a life that nourishes you. They aren't about control. They're about connection. They invite you into a relationship with your time, your energy, your essence.

To awaken is not to become someone new—it is to remember who you are beneath the layers of performance and perfection. It is not a project. It is a return. Not perfectly. Not urgently. But consciously.

Changing Your Relationship with Time

The truth is that most of life will unfold in accordance with forces far outside your control, regardless of what your mind says about it.
Michael Singer, *The Untethered Soul*

If there's one universal lament among today's professionals, it's this: *There's never enough time.*

In my years working with high-performance people, I've noticed a pattern.

Those under fifty—especially with children at home—speak of scarcity. They ask how to stretch time, hack it, squeeze more from every minute.

Those over fifty—often empty nesters—speak of wasting time. They express a persistent regret over the time they can't get back. They wish they'd used their days differently, more wisely.

Both perspectives reveal the same truth: Your relationship with time is often rooted in disempowerment, not presence.

Busy calendars may signal perceived importance, but real progress requires something counterintuitive: time to pause, reflect, and act intentionally.

Busyness masquerades as virtue. It masks avoidance and keeps you trapped in perpetual motion, and leads—over time—not just to physical exhaustion but to a chipping away of your creativity, purpose, and sense of connection.

At some point, you've likely felt the frustration of time slipping through your fingers—of evenings ending with that familiar dissatisfaction: *I wish I had more time.*

The tragedy is that these fleeting wishes often evolve into a lifetime of *If only*.

> *If only I had more hours ...*
> *If only I had gotten there sooner ...*
> *If only I had chosen differently ...*

But time itself never changes. What must change is your relationship with time.

A Client Story: Rachel Stopped Racing and Started Creating

Rachel, the global head of finance at a $100 million company, embodied everything our culture celebrates: the executive role, the impressive resume, the facade of a seemingly perfect life. On paper, she had arrived. But behind the polish, something essential had gone quiet.

"I'm always racing," she confided during one of our early sessions, "but I don't even know anymore what I'm racing toward."

That sentence held the weight of a realization long in the making. She had hit her long-coveted milestone—a role she thought would finally deliver the satisfaction she needed. But instead, she felt... empty.

Her shift didn't come from productivity hacks or better calendar management. It came from changing her relationship with time—and with herself. Rachel began to insert purposeful pauses between meetings. She stopped measuring her worth by her output. And she carved out space each morning—not to review earnings reports, but to reconnect with her breath, her body, her relationship with herself first. She intentionally slowed her pace and stopped the autopilot.

Then, something remarkable happened: As she created space in her schedule to connect with herself, her creativity returned.

Rachel, who had once loved writing fiction as a child, found her voice again. What began as calm journaling blossomed into drafting a children's book and later, publishing it.

"I thought I had to race to feel productive," she told me. "But creativity made me more productive because it made me feel whole."

Rachel didn't abandon her career. She enriched it by adding more of the right things and removing what detracted from her life. Creativity wasn't a detour or an escape. It was the bridge between doing and being.

Rethinking Time: A New Success Paradigm

In the work cultures of our modern societies, you're taught to equate productivity with importance. Busyness becomes a proxy for value. The world rewards the outward hustle and completely ignores the inner cost.

Yet, the people we most admire—the ones who move with presence, clarity, and reserved power—are rarely those sprinting from one task to the next. They're the ones who have rewritten the definition of success altogether.

True success is about how much of yourself you bring to what you choose to do. Not how many hours you grind through, but how deeply you feel alive while you're doing it.

> *True success is about how much of yourself you bring to what you choose to do.*

To feel free—connected, fulfilled, and present—is the real flex. And you don't need a new job or title to claim it. You need a new relationship with time. One that honors your energy. One that reflects your values. One that lets your creativity, your intuition, and your soul breathe.

This sense of being free isn't something you earn when you "have enough." It's not even about doing less. It's about living more deeply.

Learning from Nature: The Luna Moth

If you want to understand the cost of relentless craving—and the liberation of presence—look to one of nature's most profound teachers: the luna moth.

Its journey begins with insatiable consumption. As a caterpillar, it eats endlessly, preparing for its transformation. This consumption isn't aimless, it's purposeful. It's part of a sacred rhythm.

When the time comes, the luna moth retreats into stillness. It enters the chrysalis—silent, hidden, patient. And when it emerges, it is breathtaking: vibrant green wings and a rare, luminous presence that feels like witnessing a miracle.

The more extraordinary truth? Once it emerges, the luna moth has no mouth and cannot eat. Its purpose is no longer consumption; it's simply to live, to produce life, and to exist fully in the fleeting days it's been given.

It doesn't cling to life or crave more time. It fully inhabits each moment.

The Symbolism: A Personal Encounter

Now you know the reason for the creature on this book's cover. While writing, I had my own encounter with a luna moth that deeply touched me. One afternoon, deep in reflection at a rental house in Vermont's Green Mountains (where I was to focus on writing my initial manuscript), a luna moth landed beside me.

A creature I had never before seen now rested beside me and spent a few precious moments of its short life with me. Its vivid green wings, the softness of its form, the stillness of its presence felt like a sign from the divine. A reminder that the very transformation I was writing about wasn't about doing more, but about *being* more. More present. More at peace. More connected to nature and to what truly matters.

The luna moth found me as I was moving through my own chrysalis—shedding old cravings, releasing old structures, and stepping more deeply into my authenticity.

It wasn't just a symbol of transformation. It was a symbol of a new kind of success—one rooted in the present moment.

Choosing to Live Differently

*You are not here to merely survive your days—
you are here to fully inhabit them.*

Maya Angelou

To live from the inside out is to remember what the world taught you to forget: Your worth isn't something you earn, it's something you embody. You were never meant to endlessly chase. You were meant to become.

This doesn't mean rejecting ambition, but rooting it in something deeper. It means feeding your soul, not just your schedule. It means loosening the grip of constant striving and chasing, and instead, finding a rhythm that honors your energy, your truth, and your joy.

This choice—to live with intention—requires courage. It invites you to soften into stillness. To shed the layers of expectation that no longer fit. To trust who you're becoming, even when the destination is still unknown.

Most of all, it invites you to remember: You are already enough. You always have been.

You don't need to outrun life. You need to inhabit it.

Like the luna moth, you are not here to consume endlessly. You are here to live purposefully, with the luminous time you've been given.

This is the beginning of your return—not to who you were, but to who you've always been.

Self-Awareness Practices to Reclaim Presence

Throughout this chapter, we've explored what it means to awaken from the trance of autopilot—where routines numb our vitality, the illusion of control traps us in reactive patterns, and time itself feels like an adversary. We've named the subtle forces that keep us stuck: the beliefs that busyness equals worth, the scripts that say stillness is laziness, and the pressure to perform rather than to simply be.

The practices that follow are not merely exercises, they are antidotes to mindlessness. They reflect the central insights of this chapter:

- Awakening from mindless scheduling to meaningful presence
- Shifting your relationship with time from something to conquer to something to inhabit
- Releasing the illusion of control

When you practice these principles with intention, you begin to interrupt the mindless momentum that drains your energy and dims your light. Instead of racing through the day, you'll find moments where you are fully present and time will feel very different. Like Rachel, you can learn to make space for your well-being and find that everything changes. Instead of reacting to every pull for your attention, you'll respond from a place of choice and clarity.

This is how transformation begins—not by overhauling your life overnight, but by reclaiming your attention, your energy, and your presence, one conscious moment at a time. This is the activation of your self-awareness.

Self-Awareness Practice: Reclaim Your Attention Today

For the next week, begin each morning by asking yourself a simple but profound question:

What is the one moment today I want to be fully present for?

It could be a meaningful conversation, a home-cooked meal, a client meeting, small celebration, or your child's game or recital. Choose it deliberately. Name it. Hold space for it.

Each evening, take two minutes to reflect:

- Did I show up fully for that moment?
- If yes, how did it feel? If no, what pulled me away?

No judgment. No shame. Just awareness. You're building a life of presence moment to moment. Small hinges swing big doors.

Self-Awareness Practice: Reclaim Your Response

For the next week, when you feel emotionally triggered or overstimulated, practice the following steps:

1. Create space
   - Step away physically or mentally

2. Use the 4-7-8 breathing technique
   - Inhale through your nose for 4 seconds
   - Hold for 7 seconds

- Exhale through your mouth for 8 seconds
- Repeat for 6–8 cycles

3. Ask yourself questions to activate your presence
   - What response would reflect my values here? (It's okay if no response is your answer)
   - What does my calm, grounded self want to say or do next?

Over time, this pause becomes a source of strength—not avoidance, but empowered recalibration.

CHAPTER 2

Challenging Outdated Beliefs

*The thoughts you do not question are
the life you unconsciously create.*
Joseph Murphy, *The Power of Your Subconscious Mind*

If you want to change your life, you first have to change the way you think about it.

Sounds easy, I know, but here's the challenge: Most of your thoughts aren't new. They're echoes of old patterns—ingrained beliefs you absorbed without realizing, repeated so often they now feel like truth.

Without realizing it, you may have internalized the following beliefs that quietly dictate your choices, energy, and self-worth:

> *Success requires sacrifice.*
> *Busyness equals importance.*
> *My value is measured by how much I do.*

These aren't just harmless background noises. They're the outputs of the operating system of your life. Left unchallenged, these beliefs keep you trapped in cycles of overcommitment, self-criticism, and exhaustion—no matter how much you achieve.

Transformation starts with thinking differently and, in turn, believing differently about who you are and what you deserve.

In this chapter, we'll begin the courageous work of bravely confronting the outdated stories still driving you and replace them with truths far more empowering, authentic, and alive.

Transformation starts with **thinking differently** and, in turn, **believing differently** about who you are and what you deserve.

The True Cost of Burnout

Burnout isn't just a buzzword; it's a slow, invisible unraveling. A muted erosion of energy, creativity, and joy that happens when we've lived too long by the belief that busyness proves your worth and exhaustion is simply the price of success.

Warren Buffett once said, "It should not be a sign of success that you have no space in your [schedule]." But that's exactly what our culture celebrates: the back-to-back meetings, the packed inbox, the calendar that proves our value by leaving no room to breathe.

The data is sobering: The American Psychological Association reports that nearly 60% of professionals experience negative impacts of stress—including lack of motivation, irritability, and emotional fatigue. Stanford University links workplace stress to over 120,000 deaths each year in the US alone.

Let that land. We are sacrificing not just time—but our very lives—for an illusion of success. Busyness without intentionality isn't success. It's self-abandonment. And the tragedy is that we often don't realize we're in too deep until the damage is done. Like I mentioned in the introduction, this all happened to me too—I ignored my migraines until they evolved into fainting spells and paralyzing anxiety attacks. But this is your opportunity to interrupt the cycle earlier than I did—to reimagine productivity not as output, but as alignment.

Our minds are masterful at perpetuating stress. When we're stuck shallow breathing, barely drawing air into the belly, our bodies signal distress. The mind, ever responsive, interprets this as a threat, conjuring stressful thoughts to match. It's a vicious loop—stress in the body begets stress in the mind, and vice versa. And it all unfolds so quietly that we often don't even realize we're bracing against the very life we're meant to be living.

Fulfillment isn't measured by how much you do—it's measured by how present and alive you feel while doing it. It's time to stop measuring your days by the boxes you checked, and start measuring them by how true you were to yourself.

Moving Beyond the Need to Prove Yourself

Perfectionism is a self-destructive and addictive belief system that fuels the primary thought: If I look perfect and do everything perfectly, I can avoid or minimize the painful feelings of shame, judgment, and blame.

Brené Brown

Perfectionism. People-pleasing. Overcommitment. They all share a common belief: *We must earn our worth.*

And here's the kicker: That belief rarely starts with us. It's inherited, modeled, and rewarded. Early on, we learn the subtle, insidious lesson that approval follows performance, that love is conditional, that belonging must be purchased through relentless effort.

Benjamin—a client and a VP at a fast-growing company—had three decades of experience and a close relationship with his CEO. On paper, he was successful, respected, and secure. But self-doubt clung to him like static. Every presentation felt like an audition. Every decision, a referendum on his worth. Not because others were scrutinizing him—it was his internal script.

He wasn't being judged; he was self-judging. And his need to prove didn't bring peace. It brought paralysis. He couldn't be himself and lacked the confidence to lead as expected because he was too busy standing in his own way.

Benjamin's story isn't unique, it's a mirror. It reflects the dangerous illusion that if you just get it right—flawless enough, responsive enough, accomplished enough—you'll finally feel calm and confident inside your own life.

The truth is that **a sense of calm and confidence cannot be earned**. They require permission.

The permission to trust yourself. To choose differently. To stop performing and start leading. Because your leadership isn't defined by how flawlessly you execute. It's defined by how authentically you show up.

You don't have to do it all. You have to do what matters. You don't have to *prove* yourself. You have to **trust** yourself.

There is a vast difference between the two—and learning that difference will change your life.

The Stories You Didn't Choose but Can Change

At the root of every draining habit—every tendency to overextend, overcommit, or override your own needs—lies a belief. And not necessarily a belief you consciously chose; most often, it's one you inherited.

Somewhere along the way, long before you had the tools to question it, you inherited silent mantras:

Rest is lazy.
Saying no is selfish.
If I don't do it, it won't get done.
More is always better.

These beliefs don't announce themselves loudly, but they operate like invisible code, scripting your decisions and shaping your life until you're living a version of success that doesn't feel like your own.

The stories we tell ourselves aren't neutral—they become our operating system. But the powerful truth is that stories are made of thoughts, and thoughts can be rewritten.

Once you begin to see the beliefs that have been secretly running the show, you can't unsee them—and that *seeing* is the beginning of freedom. It's a giant leap forward.

The powerful truth is that stories are made of thoughts, and thoughts can be rewritten.

In the next section, you'll begin reconnecting with your own inner ecosystem. Not just intellectually, but viscerally. Because the stories you carry don't just live in your mind; they live in your nervous system, your breath, your body, your very choices.

It's time to tune in, listen deeply, and reclaim the pen from the narratives that no longer serve you. Onwards and upwards.

Outdated Beliefs That Keep You Stuck

It is the fact that we long for what we don't have that makes us unhappy. When we get what we longed for, we're already thinking about something new.

Lodro Rinzler, *The Buddha Walks Into a Bar*

Let's name the internal narratives—the inherited scripts—that keep even the most brilliant leaders overcommitted, spread thin, and stuck in survival mode. These beliefs are old and outdated. They were likely never yours to begin with. But they've shaped how you show up, and it's time to reclaim your agency.

Outdated Belief #1:
My success is measured by how much I do.

New Paradigm:
My success is defined by what I do with intention.

More isn't better if it costs you your health, clarity, or joy. You don't need to do it all. You need to do what's aligned with who you are.

Outdated Belief #2:
I must be constantly available.

New Paradigm:
My value is in my presence, not my proximity.

You teach others how to treat your time by how you treat it yourself. Boundaries aren't barriers—they're beacons, signaling how others can respect your energy, and how they can learn to respect their own.

Outdated Belief #3:
Busyness is a sign of importance.

New Paradigm:
Stillness is a strategy, not a liability.

Unstructured thinking time allows you to step out of the noise and busyness, creating space for deeper reflection and sharper insight. Stillness isn't idleness, it's the fertile ground where your best thinking takes root.

Outdated Belief #4:
I can (and should) do it all.

New Paradigm:
Freedom comes from focus, not from doing everything.

Overcommitment dilutes your impact. Saying no isn't weakness, it's wisdom. When you do less, but do it with purpose, your influence expands exponentially.

Outdated Belief #5:
I must prioritize others' needs to be valued.

New Paradigm:
Prioritizing myself is how I create value for others.

You can't pour from an empty cup. The more nourished you are, the more energy you have to give, and the more authentically and powerfully you can show up for others.

These outdated beliefs may have shaped your past, but they don't have to define your future.

What defines you now is your awareness—your ability to see these old scripts for what they are. It's the courage to say, "This story no longer serves me and I'm ready to live differently."

That's not selfish. That's sovereignty. That's how you begin to lead—yourself and others—from a place of wholeness.

Awareness is the first courageous act. Once you've named the belief, the next step is to rewrite it. To consciously choose a new narrative that reflects the life **you want to live**—not the one you were conditioned to accept.

From Erin's Journey: How I Unwound My Outdated Beliefs

Before I could empower others, I had to confront these outdated beliefs in myself. I didn't just name them—I *lived* them.

For years, I measured my worth by how much I could cram into a day. I believed that busyness made me important, that being constantly available made me indispensable, that saying yes to everything was the price of success. I relentlessly sought validation through productivity and people-pleasing.

These beliefs weren't conscious at first. They were ingrained coping strategies for self-doubt and a subtle undercurrent of unworthiness. They were patterns handed down by a culture that equates doing with worth and self-sacrifice with value. I was excelling in my corporate roles, delivering results, climbing the ladder. But behind the polished facade was a continual emptiness. I was exhausted, reactive, and disconnected—from myself, from my loved ones, from life.

The first shift came when I realized that *more* wasn't making me feel better. It was making me resentful, burned out, perpetually behind where I truly wanted to be. I began experimenting with small, intentional pauses: breathing before replying to an email, taking midday walks, creating silent space in the mornings and evenings. These moments felt almost rebellious, but they cracked open a space of clarity and presence I hadn't known in years.

I had to confront the guilt that surfaced when I set boundaries. I believed that prioritizing myself would make me selfish or less committed. But as I practiced honoring my own needs, I discovered a paradox: My presence—when grounded and intentional—was far more impactful than any amount of frantic overfunctioning. My leadership deepened. My relationships strengthened. My decisions became clearer. My intuition heightened.

This wasn't a quick fix; it was a gradual unlearning. I rewrote the outdated scripts one discerning moment, one boundary, one conscious breath at a time. I learned to listen to myself, not the noise of external expectations. And in that listening, I realized: I didn't have to choose between professional success and personal fulfillment. I could have both. Not by doing more, but by doing what aligned with who I wanted to be, which is the core of *I Can Fit That In*.

A Deeper Excavation

For a couple of years before I launched my business full time, I had been quietly following the signs—saying yes to opportunities to share my perspective and passion for growth and development. I was invited to speak at company events and team retreats, and with each experience, something stirred within me. But I kept telling myself, "There's no way I can leave the stability of my corporate career and start my own business."

That belief felt so real ... but it wasn't true.

When I dug deeper, I uncovered the real root—it wasn't a fear of failure, but the fear of not being wanted, of not being worthy. And that belief had been driving my choices for years.

Here's how the excavation unfolded in my journal:

> Why can't I leave corporate?
> *Because I'm scared I won't be good enough on my own.*
>
> Is that 100% true?
> *No.*
>
> Then what's the real fear?
> *That I'll be rejected. That no one will want what I offer.*
>
> And what would that mean?
> *That I failed. That I should've stayed where I was validated.*
>
> And what does validation give me?
> *A sense of worth.*
>
> **And what if I already am worthy, without needing to prove anything?**

That was the moment I stopped letting fear drive my decisions and started consciously empowering myself to believe differently. I realized I had something unique to offer the world—insights, experience, a deep passion for helping others reclaim their lives—and I wasn't willing to keep it locked behind someone else's idea of safety.

I had to get honest about what was really holding me back: not a lack of ability or desire, but the muted influence of unworthiness. I had to shift that story.

So, I began taking small, inspired steps—not to prove, but to become. Each action was a vote for the woman I was choosing to be. The fear didn't vanish, but the momentum of my aligned choices made it irrelevant.

The deeper I dug, the more I saw that these outdated beliefs were the very ground I'd been standing on. I had to name them, face them, and consciously step off that shaky ground onto something solid. This wasn't just about changing my mind. It was about changing my life.

If I could shift these beliefs for myself—if I could reimagine what was possible and believe better—I knew others could too. And with that knowing, a new kind of courage took root. Not just for me, but for everyone ready to reclaim their story.

Self-Awareness Practice to Think Differently

The beliefs that come from fear drain us; the beliefs that come from love energize and expand us.

Don Miguel Ruiz, *The Four Agreements*

Throughout this chapter, you've courageously surfaced the invisible beliefs that have quietly shaped your life—beliefs passed down, absorbed, and repeated until they felt like your truth. You've recognized how these internal narratives have kept you tethered to overcommitment, self-doubt, and exhaustion, even when your life, on the outside, appeared successful.

Many of the old stories you carry—from inherited expectations to self-imposed pressures—are discreetly directing your choices, draining your vitality, and distancing you from your authentic self. The following self-awareness practice matters because it disrupts those patterns. It invites you to excavate and question what no longer serves you, to rewrite the narrative with intention, and to anchor your life in beliefs that nourish rather than deplete.

But awareness alone isn't the destination, it's the doorway.

The real transformation begins when you move from simply noticing outdated beliefs to consciously choosing new ones, when you interrupt autopilot with curiosity, and when you begin to live as though your energy, presence, and truth are non-negotiable.

By engaging with this practice, you'll begin to do the following:

- Recognize when fear-based beliefs try to run the show
- Create intentional space between thought and reaction
- Ground yourself in clarity and presence
- Reclaim your energy, your decisions, and your power to author your own story

Self-Awareness Practice: Excavating and Rewriting Your Inner Story

This practice invites you to identify your hidden narratives, rewrite them with intention, and anchor the new narratives in your daily life—replacing old scripts of pressure and proving, with new stories of presence and permission.

For the next week, carve out five to ten minutes each evening to engage with this practice.

Evening Reflection: Excavating and Rewriting

1. Reflect on the day
   - Where did I feel internal pressure to do more, say yes, or prove myself today? (Notice the moments of tension, racing thoughts, or reactionary agreements.)

2. Identify the underlying belief
   - Examples: *If I don't do this, I'll disappoint them. If I slow down, I'll fall behind. If I say no, I'll seem selfish.*

3. Be honest with yourself about the underlying belief
   - Is that belief absolutely true, or is it an inherited story I'm ready to change?

4. Reframe it into a new truth
   - Write the old belief and beneath it, craft an empowering truth.
   Old belief: *I must prove my worth by doing more.*
   New truth: **My worth is inherent; I do not need to earn it.**

5. Visualize your future self living this new truth
   - How does my body feel? How do my relationships shift? How does my work flow differently when it's aligned with my values?

6. Anchor the new truth
   - Speak the new truth aloud, feeling it resonate in your body.
   - Write it somewhere visible to ground your intention throughout the following days.

By the end of one week, you'll have five to seven new beliefs to visually see and internally recite to remind yourself of the truth you're discovering.

CHAPTER 3

Rewiring Your Mindset

When you stop being loyal to your old limits, your new life begins.
Neale Donald Walsch

You've started to notice your patterns. You've begun questioning the old stories that shaped your actions, choices, and even your sense of self. Now it's time to take the next step: To meet yourself beyond the noise of the mind and begin rewiring your mindset for a life of authentic, sustainable empowerment.

But before you can rewire anything, you need to create space. A cluttered, chaotic mind doesn't build new pathways. It repeats the old ones. This is the deeper meaning of "out with the old, in with the new." Not just in your closet or the junk drawers in your kitchen (though clearing those can help too), but in the mental frameworks that have shaped your choices for years.

Stillness isn't absence; it's fertile ground. New thoughts, new possibilities, and new power don't grow in noise; they grow in the intentional pause.

Freedom Begins in the Mind

When you start observing your thoughts—without judgment—you discover something liberating:

You are not your thoughts. You are the one who notices them.

They're not facts. Just patterns—echoes of past experiences, fears, and inherited programming passed down from your ancestors. They don't persist because they're true; they persist because they're familiar. And the moment you recognize them as such, you loosen their grip.

> *You are not your thoughts. You are the one who notices them.*

That is the beginning of freedom.

Freedom isn't about silencing your mind—that's not feasible. Freedom comes from choosing which thoughts to nourish and which to let go. You're no longer surviving your mind. You're leading it. And from that empowered place, you can begin building a life rooted in freedom, presence, and power.

You Are Not Your Old Patterns

The greatest limits in your life aren't imposed by the world around you. They're the quiet assumptions you've absorbed and accepted as truth—often without even realizing it.

If you've read my story in the introduction, you know I grew up amid instability and insecurity. My early environments were defined by lack, scarcity, terminal illness, and chronic stress. But I made a conscious decision: Those conditions would not define my identity. Poverty wasn't me. Illness wasn't me. The emotional chaos I inherited wasn't me.

They were the conditions I was born into, not the truth of who I was becoming. What I didn't realize until later was that these scripts weren't just mine. They were generational—woven through family patterns, cultural expectations, and ancestral conditioning. They were inherited stories of what it means to succeed, to survive, to belong. But just because they were passed down doesn't mean they're your destiny.

If I can challenge and rewrite those narratives—if I can shift from survival into sovereignty—you can too.

We all carry stories. We all carry pain, patterns, and beliefs from our upbringing, our culture, and our experiences. But none of those define you, unless you let them.

You are not these old patterns. You are the one with the power to evolve beyond them.

A Client Story: Brad's Realization

Brad, a principal at a rapidly scaling private equity firm, was revered by everyone in the organization. His colleagues described him as brilliant, loyal, and unwaveringly dependable. In private interviews, his peers, direct reports, and even the most senior partners spoke glowingly of his work ethic and character. Brad had been there since the company's early days, his fingerprints on many of its successes. From the outside, it looked like he was poised for Partner or a C-suite executive title in a portfolio company.

But inside, Brad was secretly unraveling.

Each promotion he received, rather than reinforcing his confidence, deepened his self-doubt. He found himself overpreparing for meetings, obsessing over details, and mentally rehearsing conversations days in advance and long after they'd ended. What paralyzed him wasn't the complexity of his work—it was the belief that he needed to embody the style of the head Partner, Jim, perfectly: stoic, authoritative, and seemingly bulletproof.

In coaching sessions, Brad admitted he often stayed at the office late or went back to work on his computer after his kids were asleep, not because the work demanded it, but because he felt he couldn't shut things down until he had "covered every angle." His fear that a single misstep would expose him as not enough was deep. This was a draining routine he had gotten himself into and it was taking a toll on his relationship with his wife.

He wasn't just performing for his superiors—he was performing for himself.

The weight of his internal script—*If I don't get this exactly right, I'll be exposed as not good enough*—was crushing. Even in group coaching sessions with his leadership team, Brad's contributions were often muted. He held back, fearing his ideas might not be polished enough, or that speaking up might invite scrutiny.

What was most striking was that Brad's fears weren't grounded in reality. No one around him expected perfection. In fact, his colleagues admired his insight and craved his authentic input. But Brad couldn't see that. His internal narrative was louder than any external validation. He knew exactly where it stemmed from: having been a smaller kid who had tried hard to be liked. Over time, he had taught himself that being likeable meant being more like others—and anything but himself.

About six months into our one-to-one coaching, Brad finally confronted this blind spot. During a particularly honest session, he admitted: "I'm terrified of being seen as flawed. I don't want to disappoint anyone—not my boss, not my team, not even my family. So I try to be perfect—or at least more like Jim who is close to perfect in my eyes. But it's suffocating me."

That admission was a breakthrough. We then designed purposeful rituals to help Brad reconnect with himself:

- **No longer working late at night.** Creating a hard stop to honor his well-being.
- **Choosing to connect with his wife.** Having an intentional conversation or watching a show together.
- **Being fully present with his kids.** Carving out time for connection instead of collapsing into exhaustion.
- **Practicing deep breathing before presentations.** Calming his nervous system and shifting from panic to grounded presence.
- **Eating a nutritious lunch mindfully.** No more skipping meals during work or rushing through a processed meal.
- **Journaling.** Blocking off time in his schedule once a week for strategic thinking.
- **Re-introducing his love of running.** Giving his body and mind the endorphin release it craved.

These small acts, which he practiced consistently, became his lifeline back to himself. Slowly, his grip on perfection loosened. He found peace through self-acceptance. His confidence grew because he stopped needing to get everything "right."

Over time, Brad started showing up differently. He voiced his opinions in meetings without overpreparing. He trusted his instincts. He led not by mimicking Jim's style, but by leaning into his own thoughtful, approachable, and quietly impactful style. His colleagues noticed the shift. They described him as more real, effective, and decisive.

The real transformation wasn't external, it was internal. Brad rewrote the narrative that had been driving him:

From *I must be perfect to be valued* to **My value comes from who I am, not what I produce.**

From *I need to anticipate everything* to **I trust myself to handle whatever comes in the moment.**

His story became a powerful reminder that no amount of external validation can silence an internal narrative of inadequacy. But with intentional awareness and consistent practice, those narratives can be rewritten.

Brad's journey wasn't about becoming fearless or flawless. It was about becoming free.

Unexamined thoughts become the architecture of your mind. They shape how you lead, how you love, how you live.

You are not obligated to follow beliefs that no longer reflect who you are becoming. Your life doesn't have to be directed by outdated scripts running on autopilot.

Transformation is not dramatic. The first step is awareness—seeing the thought. The second step is choice—discerning what to keep and what to release.

Your Mind Garden: Cultivating the Thoughts That Nourish You

The mind is a fertile garden—it will grow anything you wish to plant—beautiful flowers or weeds. Do not allow negative thoughts to enter your mind, for they are the weeds that strangle confidence.

Bruce Lee

Imagine your mind as a vast, living garden. Every thought you entertain, every belief you revisit, is a seed you plant. Some seeds root themselves in fear, self-doubt, and judgment, spreading thorny vines that silently choke your potential. Others blossom into clarity, trust, and creativity, nourishing your life from the inside out.

What most people never fully grasp is that you are the gardener.

You may not have chosen all the seeds first planted in your mind, since many were sown in childhood and inherited from your family, culture, or systems that were never designed with your flourishing in mind. But now, you hold the trowel. Now, you decide what gets nurtured and what gets uprooted.

This is the power of intentional self-awareness: You choose what grows.

When left untended, the mind defaults to its most familiar grooves—old conditioning, limiting beliefs, and reflexive fears. A study published in *Science* revealed that the average person's mind wanders nearly 47% of the time, and when it does, they report feeling significantly less happy than when fully present, regardless of the activity.

This mental overgrowth shows up in a number of ways:

- Chronic self-doubt and hesitation
- Internalized pressure to over-perform
- Automatic reactivity and defensiveness
- Scarcity-based thinking and fear of lack
- Inherited shame and unworthiness

Here's the challenge: The mind doesn't default to optimism or possibility. It skews to the negative—anticipating danger, guarding against disappointment, repeating old scripts of fear and criticism. If you don't consciously feed it with life-affirming, empowering beliefs, they won't get there by accident. The default wiring is based on survival. Your intentional rewiring is what rewrites the code.

A man once asked a gardener why his plants grew so beautifully. The gardener said: "I don't force them to grow, I remove what stops them."

Like a garden overrun with weeds, neglecting the mind can leave it tangled and daunting. But that doesn't mean it's beyond redemption. It means the first step is presence. The second is compassion.

Because transformation doesn't begin with a machete—it begins with noticing.

From Erin's Journey: Naming My Inner Critic

This awareness transformed my life, starting with a deceptively simple practice: I named my inner critic.

I called her "Erica."

And she's still around. In fact, Craig and I have made her an inside joke—whenever I start second-guessing myself out loud, we laugh at how hard Erica is trying.

For years, her voice dominated my mind—chattering about everything I wasn't doing, cautioning me against risks, whispering fears of *not enough* and *what ifs*. She was loud, persistent, and relentless. She'd act out—the shadow side of me—projecting fears outward, sabotaging my own efforts. It was as if life couldn't stay good for too long; Erica would start spinning the narrative that something had to go wrong, planting seeds of doubt where there was none.

But from the day I named her, something shifted. I realized: I'm not a passenger in this vehicle—I'm the driver. Erica is just along for the ride, and she's certainly not riding shotgun anymore.

Naming her gave me distance. When she flared up, I could say, "I see you. I hear your fearful voice. But you don't get to lead today." Over time, her voice didn't disappear, but it grew softer, less convincing.

Naming my inner critic didn't just diminish her power, it amplified my inner truth. I began to hear a deeper voice within me: something steady, grounded, and compassionate. It was the voice of my heart and intuition.

This is the essence of rewiring: not eradicating the inner critic, but learning to turn down its volume and amplify your authentic voice. With practice, it will lose its grip. It will still appear, but you'll meet it with awareness, not obedience.

Rewiring Your Inner Dialogue: The Language That Shapes Your Life

Once you begin to see the outdated narratives shaping your decisions, powerful truths emerge:

- You are not bound to these old stories.
- You are not obligated to obey every familiar script.
- You get to choose the inner dialogue that shapes your reality.

These may seem minute, though they are not minor shifts. They are neural rewrites—literal new wavelengths of thought that begin to reroute the autopilot patterns in your brain. The incremental change they create is powerful.

Every time you say, *I can't*, your nervous system tightens and your consciousness contracts. Every time you say, **I'm learning** or **I'm open**, your nervous system relaxes and your consciousness expands.

Words are not passive. They are energetic blueprints—frequencies that shape your inner experience and create the architecture of your life.

Language as Creation

Every time you say, *I have to*, you reinforce a narrative of obligation. Every time you say, **I choose**, you reclaim your agency.

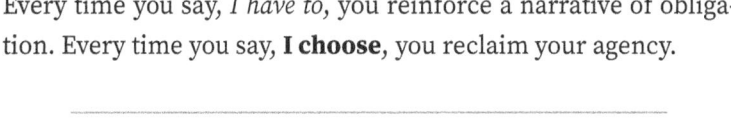

You are not the voice in your head. You are the one who listens to it.

Your words are not just descriptors of your life; they're designers of it. You are not the voice in your head. You are the one who listens to it.

The language you use shapes your reality, moment by moment. With each phrase, you either reinforce old stories or write new ones. For example:

- Instead of *I'm behind*, try **I'm aligned with what matters**.
- Instead of *I'll never figure this out*, say **I'm learning as I go**.
- Instead of *I'm not enough*, affirm **I am already whole**.
- Replace *I have to do this* with **I choose to do this**.
- Shift from *I should do that* to **I may do that**.

More than semantics, these are micro-decisions that shape your mindset and influence your emotions, energy, and outcomes.

Dr. James Doty at Stanford University reminds us that intentional practices like reframing and visualization create new neural pathways—neuroplasticity in action. Your brain is always listening, always ready to rewire itself based on the messages you feed it.

The more you practice new, empowering language, the more you shift your internal state. And when you shift your internal state, you change your life.

This isn't just anecdotal wisdom, it's backed by science. In the Neuroscience for Business course at MIT Sloan's executive management school, which I completed during the pandemic, Dr. Tara Swart shared a compelling insight: Leaders who consciously reframe setbacks (even perceived) as opportunities for growth not only enhance their resilience and decision-making capabilities but also strengthen their emotional intelligence. By viewing challenges as learning experiences, they don't just improve themselves, they create a culture of continuous improvement and authenticity.

This science-backed perspective underscores an essential truth: Rewiring your mind isn't about silencing every negative thought, but transforming your relationship with those thoughts. You consciously decide which stories you'll amplify, and which you'll release.

Reclaiming Your Inner Authority: Leading from Within

You were never meant to be led by fear, outdated narratives, or the endless chase for approval. You were meant to lead yourself—from within.

Your spirit is your truth; it knows the way and is your compass. Reclaiming your inner authority is to reconnect with the quiet, steady power that's always been within you. It's remembering that life isn't something to manage, it's something to be present in with clarity and self-trust. And trusting yourself isn't a luxury; it's the foundation for fulfillment and self-actualization.

This is a way of being. Noticing when you start to hand over your power is how you stop looking to others for permission and validation and start listening to the truth within. It sounds like this:

> **I choose how I show up today, no matter what others expect.**
> **I trust what I know, even if no one else sees it yet.**
> **I am the author of my next chapter.**

I know what it feels like to silence yourself. It happened to me in ordinary moments—sitting in a boardroom, surrounded by sharp minds and strong opinions. I knew I had something important to say, something bold and necessary. But I hesitated. My inner critic flooded my mind with doubt:

> *What if this sounds naive?*
> *What if this isn't what they want to hear?*
> *What if I'm wrong?*
> *How will they react? What will they think of me?*

In those moments, I didn't just silence an idea—I handed over my authority. I deferred to fear. Erica took the wheel, steering me into silence.

This is where so many of us, men and women alike, fall into the trap of imposter tendencies. We stay silent thinking we're protecting ourselves and avoiding rejection or humiliation. And over time, this becomes autopilot—our default reaction to any situation where we have something to say but hear the voice of doubt.

The real cost is that when you're not true to yourself—when you withhold your authentic expression—you're not being true to others. They're getting a different version of you and can sense that your words or behaviors are disingenuous. If that's the case, they'll treat you differently because their own inner authority will tell them not to trust you. That's why you feel like an imposter or you don't belong. And while it's easy to blame others for not recognizing your value, the deeper truth is that you're the one silencing your own voice.

When I started noticing how easily I abandoned myself in the name of belonging, comfort, or approval, I made a promise: No more outsourcing my voice or worth. Reclaiming my inner authority wasn't about speaking louder or taking up more space. It was about standing firmly in who I already was, and letting my actions flow from that grounded clarity.

I made a promise: No more outsourcing my voice or worth.

We were all born with an inner authority. As children, we spoke from instinct, heart, and truth. We were deeply connected to our human spirit and it shined through us brightly. But over time, conditioned by expectations—parents, teachers, bosses, culture, society—we learned to perform, prove, and please. The inner critic grew louder as the authentic voice quieter. Approval-seeking replaced self-trust.

The good news is this pattern can be broken. Not by fighting it (resistance only makes it stronger), but by noticing it. By pausing and asking, "Is this really true for me?" If the answer is no, you don't have to listen. You can choose differently. Micro-decisions, made in moments of self-awareness, begin the shift back to your own knowing.

This is your reconnection. Not a call to effort, but a call to presence. Not about doing more, but about becoming more yourself.

Principles for Re-Centering Yourself

Before we transition into self-awareness practices, consider these principles as living invitations. They're pathways back to your center, not tasks to check off. Think of them as the fertile soil where your daily practices can take root and grow. These require no extra time, they're simply taking place within your own mind as you direct your thoughts. When integrated over time, this way of directing your mind will become natural and your old ways will become more distant. These principles won't just change how you manage your days, they'll transform how you lead your life.

Pause Before You React
Before replying to that email or agreeing to that request, ask yourself, "Am I responding from my truth or from old conditioning?" This pause is a micro-moment of sovereignty and a space where you can choose clarity over reflex.

Speak Even When It Feels Uncomfortable
Your voice matters—even when it trembles. Every time you honor your truth, you strengthen the bridge back to yourself. Integrity is built in these small moments of courageous expression.

Define Success on Your Terms—Daily
Each morning, choose a word that embodies your version of success: Presence. Clarity. Grace. Boldness. Let it guide your decisions. Let it anchor you in a definition of success that aligns with your truth, not with external expectations.

Reflect with Compassion, Not Criticism
At the end of the week, ask yourself, "Where did I honor my truth? Where did I abandon it?" This reflection is for recalibration, not judgment. It's a loving return to yourself, a gentle course correction back into alignment.

These are acts of devotion to the self you're no longer willing to betray. To the leader within you who chooses alignment over performance at any expense. To the person you trust to lead your life—not just in public, but in the still, unseen moments. Like on a rainy day and the cart return is ten spots away.

Self-Awareness Practice for Cultivating Clarity and Self-Trust

As we saw in Brad's story, before you can fully reclaim your inner authority—before you can lead your life from alignment rather than old scripts and borrowed expectations—you must begin with one essential act: listening to yourself.

The practice that follows isn't about fixing you, performing better, or ticking another box. It's an invitation to pause, notice, and reconnect with the muffled wisdom already within you. Designed to help you turn down the noise of inherited patterns and turn up the volume on your own truth, this tool creates space for a profound internal shift. This is inner work.

When practiced consistently, it does more than shift isolated thoughts. It initiates a deep reorientation of your inner world, laying the mental and emotional foundation where self-trust can thrive, clarity flows naturally, and your mind and heart move in coherence. In time, you'll notice your thoughts, feelings, words, and actions begin to align—vibrating together, rhythmically dancing through life in a masterful flow.

It guides you into a life where

- your inner dialogue supports rather than sabotages you,
- your choices reflect alignment rather than reaction,
- your presence becomes your true power.

Remember: This isn't about achieving something or chasing perfection, but cultivating presence—moment by moment and breath by breath—until presence becomes your natural way of being: the quiet yet profound result of your commitment to yourself.

Self-Awareness Practice: Cultivating Your Inner Garden of Thought

For the next week, try this simple yet transformative ritual.

Morning: Plant the Seed

- Get still. Place your hand on your heart. Breathe deeply.
- Choose one empowering quality—trust, calm, courage, clarity, joy, peace, abundance.
- Set your intention:
  - Today, I choose to nourish [chosen quality].
  - Today, I move through my day anchored in [chosen quality].

Throughout the Day: Tend the Garden

- When a fear-based or limiting thought arises, pause.
- Name it: old story, self-doubt, scarcity.
- Gently redirect:
  - Today, I am cultivating [chosen quality].

Evening: Reflect and Recalibrate

- Ask yourself,
  - What thoughts did I nourish today?
  - What old patterns did I notice but chose not to water?
  - How did aligning with my chosen quality shift my experience—my decisions, energy, and presence?
- Reflect on a moment where you felt your inner authority strengthen—a moment where you chose yourself over a familiar pattern.

This is a series of small, daily acts of self-leadership that, when woven together, create profound transformation—from the inside out.

CHAPTER 4

Reigniting Your Inner Spark

When we are no longer able to change a situation, we are challenged to change ourselves.

Viktor Frankl, *Man's Search for Meaning*

In a culture that glorifies the hustle and grind, celebrates performance at any cost, and normalizes depletion, choosing to feel alive isn't indulgence, it's strategy.

Your inner spark isn't some soft or abstract notion, it's your power source. It's a vital indicator of your energy, creativity, and capacity to lead and live in a way that's both sustainable and soulfully aligned. When you're lit from within, you don't just feel better, you lead better. You generate energy rather than drain it. You create from alignment, not exhaustion.

So, let me ask you a question that few people in your professional circle likely have:

What makes you a gift to this world?

And I mean this genuinely. Every soul carries a unique brilliance, a light that was never meant to be dimmed. It's not your title. It's not how much you can multi-task, which revenue targets you can hit, or how many unread notifications you can survive.

It's your presence. Your essence. The energy you bring into a room when you're fully alive—not just functional.

That light has always lived inside you. But somewhere along the way, it was dimmed—first by the expectations of others (even those with supportive families and seemingly idyllic childhoods unconsciously absorb familial, cultural, and societal programming). And then, more subtly, by the voice in your own head whispering:

> *Do more.*
> *Prove yourself.*
> *Don't slow down.*

But what if, right now, you gave yourself permission to stop dimming and start designing?

The Happiest People You Know Want Less and Live More

Picture the happiest person you actually know—not someone curated on Instagram, but someone whose presence feels light, grounded, and unmistakably alive. Someone with a quiet strength and kindness, whose company leaves you feeling at ease and uplifted.

What do you notice?

- They work and live fully, but they're not chasing everything or constantly striving.
- They're not sprinting through life on adrenaline or the approval of others.
- They move with a calm confidence that comes from alignment, not overachievement.

You've likely encountered this energy in someone at work, in your community, or within your network—someone who exudes contentment and clarity. Employees and leaders with a strong sense of purpose and fulfillment are more resilient, less prone to burnout, and significantly more effective under pressure. Their joy doesn't come from having more; it comes from being more connected to what truly matters.

The You Who Already Knows

You carry the wisdom of two powerful guides: your younger self and your future self.

Your younger self—especially your wildly imaginative, unfiltered seven-to-nine-year-old self—didn't care about LinkedIn endorsements, Instagram likes, or quarterly KPIs. He or she simply followed what lit them up, with a fearless willingness to try even when failure was inevitable. Back then, you didn't look at a masterpiece and think, *I'll never be able to do that, so why bother?* You didn't say no to little league because you doubted you'd make the major leagues.

You carry the wisdom of two powerful guides: your younger self and your future self.

Pause and ask yourself, "What did I love doing before the world told me who to be?"

Write down three to five memories when you felt fully alive—whether you were storytelling, building, creating, exploring, or connecting.

Then ask, "Where are those threads in my life today? If they're missing, how might I begin to revive them?"

Even a small act—picking up a paintbrush, taking a walk without a destination, moving the pen in a journal, or leading a meeting from the heart—can reignite your spark. Creativity does something miraculous: It activates the right hemisphere of your brain, the part connected to your heart and emotions. It invites you to feel rather than just think, shifting you out of the brain's central fear response and into presence and possibility.

Now, turn to your future self—the wise, discerning eighty-year-old you who has already lived the story you're still writing. This version of you knows what truly matters.

Pause and ask your future self these important questions:

- What choices brought me the most joy?
- What did I wish I'd said yes to sooner?
- What do I wish I'd released earlier?

I revisited this exercise about six months after returning from Bali. By then, I had been living by the philosophy I now teach: ritualizing what matters, designing my days with intention rather than autopilot, and turning down the volume of external noise. In that stillness—and through the very tools I'm guiding you through—a deeper voice emerged. The voice of the woman I was becoming. She didn't speak loudly or rush. She was calm, centered, and clear.

What she told me was simple but seismic: **You don't have to keep living a life that no longer fits. You can choose to live a life that feels aligned with who you truly are.**

I stopped outsourcing permission. I stopped performing for approval. I began honoring the wisdom that had always been within me, and letting her lead.

And in time, something miraculous happened. I found myself excited to wake up each day. I went from a reticent sigh of *Ugh, I have to do it all over again* to **I can't wait to see what today brings.** It was a shift in mindset that rippled through every aspect of my life, transforming my mood, my energy, and my outlook.

Realignment is the result of calling back the parts of yourself you've left behind, and integrating the wisdom of who you're becoming.

Stepping Into the Unknown: Where Growth Begins

As you listen to the quiet wisdom of your younger and future selves, you'll likely feel a subtle pull—the tug of the familiar. The mind loves what it knows—the safe, the predictable, the rehearsed. But growth doesn't live there.

The path of least resistance—the known—might feel comfortable, but it's constrictive. It limits your expansion. Our souls didn't come here just to play it safe; we came to evolve. And that evolution isn't a mental exercise—it's an energetic unfolding sensed from within, not from external achievement. Ironically, it's this inner shift that often opens the door to external abundance and expansion.

The edge of your comfort zone is where curiosity heightens, where creativity sparks, and where life reawakens.

In the executive workshops I run, I often encourage a simple yet powerful practice: Adopt a beginner's mindset. Enter each situation—a conversation, a challenge, a personal aspiration—as if you know nothing. Even when you do. Let go of assumptions and ask yourself the basic questions:

- What if I approached this differently?
- What if I didn't already know the outcome?
- What if I let wonder lead me instead of fear?

When you meet life with the open mind of a beginner, the ego becomes silent and the heart awakens. This isn't naivety, it's intentional vulnerability. It's the space where possibility expands.

There's a reason people say the longest journey is the twelve inches from your head to your heart. True wisdom doesn't live in intellectual analysis alone. It lives in the integration of thought and feeling—in the courage to act on the quiet guidance within.

When you step beyond the familiar, you shift from playing it safe to engaging with the world as a co-creator of your experience. At the edge of your comfort zone lies the learning zone, and beyond that, the growth zone.

The journey is in leaning into the discomfort that transforms you—journeying inward, not just forward.

Clarifying Your Core Values and Aspirations

Most people don't burn out solely because they're doing too much. They burn out because they're doing too much of what no longer aligns with who they are.

Values misalignment is one of the most insidious sources of exhaustion. McKinsey & Company reports that employees whose personal values align with their organization's are four times more engaged and five times more likely to experience consistent well-being. And yet, many high performers stay loyal to roles, relationships, or expectations that secretly erode their spirit. Why? Because they've never stopped long enough to ask themselves, "What do I truly value?"

This isn't your boss's job—or anyone else's—to figure out for you. As you evolve, it's up to you to first get radically honest with yourself about how your values may have shifted (because they do and will throughout your life) or where new misalignments are covertly draining your energy. It may mean you have to have the necessary, and uncomfortable, conversations to make a change.

But many people don't. They stay in relationships because they convince themselves it's easier than leaving. They stay in jobs for fear of letting someone down, feeling like a failure, or dreading the hard work of starting over. They remain tethered to friendships or social groups that have worn out their welcome, draining rather than energizing them, because they believe it's better to stay than to risk being alone. But in doing so, they're devaluing themselves—settling for a status quo that no longer fits.

I wasn't brave about living by my own values for years. Like many high achievers, I equated success with performance, recognition, and pushing through. But as my self-awareness deepened, I began to notice a widening gap between who I was becoming and the world I was still trying to fit into.

I remember one deal that crystallized this truth. After being pressured to include someone on a client project—someone who had barely contributed and nearly jeopardized the deal but wanted half the commission—I felt an initial wave of fury. But instead of reacting from anger, I paused, breathed, and responded from grounded self-respect. I calmly advocated for fairness in the commission split, which eventually required arbitration by upper management. While I didn't get everything I believed was fair, I stood with my integrity intact. That person quit soon after, and I suspect management realized they might have awarded him less had they anticipated his exit.

That moment taught me a valuable lesson: You can be successful, kind, and assertive without betraying your values or giving away your power.

As my friend and author Alison Fragale says, you can be a *Likeable Badass*.

> *You can be successful, kind, and assertive without betraying your values or giving away your power.*

The ones who lead from ego might win the short-term game. But we're living in a time of shift, where egotistical behaviors and outdated power dynamics are losing their grip. The long game belongs to those who lead from alignment.

Define What Matters to You

Let's do this together. Pause and ask yourself, "What are my top five core values?"

(Not the ones you think you should have—the ones that truly light you up, ground you, and make you feel most alive.)

Not sure where to start? Consider this list of core values as a springboard, and feel free to explore Brené Brown's *Dare to Lead List of Values* or Jim Collins' *Built to Last* for deeper reflection:

Accountability	Creativity	Loyalty
Adaptability	Curiosity	Passion
Appreciation	Dependability	Respect
Authenticity	Empathy	Spirituality
Compassion	Excellence	Trust
Connection	Honesty	Vision
Courage	Integrity	Wisdom

Then ask yourself, "Where am I already honoring these values? Where am I betraying them?"

Too often, we stay loyal to roles, expectations, or relationships while stealthily betraying ourselves. That's not noble. It's a slow erosion of your energy and truth.

The spark you once knew and you're seeking to reignite isn't gone, it's just been dimmed under the weight of expectations, overextension, and self-abandonment. But it's still there, waiting for you to turn toward it.

What if today, you gave yourself full permission to move through life with purpose and a deep sense of belonging—to yourself? What if you felt proud, not just of what you've achieved, but of who you're becoming?

And what if it felt … great?

Self-Awareness Practice to Reignite Your Light from Within

Your inner spark isn't something to find, it's something to remember. This chapter has guided you to the wisdom of your younger and future selves, invited you to honor your truth, and encouraged you to identify and realign with your core values. Now, it's time to shift from insight to action.

This tool is an invitation to pause, recalibrate, and reconnect. It offers a moment of conscious return—from mindless doing to meaningful being. It's designed to help you step into alignment, reawaken your vitality, and lead from your power.

When practiced consistently, these tools will help you

- tune in to the energy that fuels you, and recognize what depletes you,
- align your daily actions with your deepest values,
- create small but powerful moments of clarity, integrity, and intention.

Self-Awareness Practice: Tuning In to Your Well-Being

Reigniting your spark begins with a kind, honest scan of your whole self. This practice invites you to gently assess your energy, not to judge or fix anything, but to listen to what your mind, body, heart, and spirit are trying to tell you.

The Well-Being Reflection

On a scale of 1 to 5 (1 = disconnected, unsatisfied, or depleted; 5 = vibrant, fulfilled, or consistent), rate how you currently feel in each of these five domains:

- Mental
- Emotional
- Physical
- Spiritual
- Relational

Then, ask yourself,

- Where do I feel most vibrant and alive?
- Where do I feel depleted, neglected, or stretched thin?
- Which area has been quietly calling for my attention?

These areas aren't problems to fix, they're invitations to take notice, to listen deeply, and to gently shift your mindset and actions. Use your reflection as a touchstone to realign, and revisit this practice anytime you feel off-center or misaligned.

You don't have to turn your life upside down to find peace within. It begins with small, deliberate acts of tuning in and taking inspired action on what you hear.

PART 2

TRANSFORMING YOUR LIFE THROUGH RITUALS

Rituals: Living Structures That Align

Discipline is remembering what you want.
David Campbell

Part 1 brought you back to your truth. You cleared the noise, shed outdated beliefs, and reconnected with what lights you up. Now, in part 2, it's time to root that truth into your daily life, not by bolting back into hustle, but by weaving a new rhythm: a way of living that honors who you are now, not just who you used to be. Part 1 helped you remember what truly matters, and part 2 invites you to reimagine how you live.

Rituals aren't simply upgraded habits. Rituals are intentional, rhythmic choices that nourish your presence, restore your energy, and elevate how you show up in your work, your relationships, and your life. Where routines ask, "What needs to get done?" rituals ask, "What do I want this to mean?"

At the end of each chapter in part 2, you'll find a realignment ritual section. Like the self-awareness practices of part 1, these sections are where you're invited to apply the lessons of the chapter to your own life and build your own rituals.

Your rituals are uniquely yours. They evolve as you do. They become the living architecture of a life that reflects who you are.

We begin here—not by adding more, but by choosing with intention—to live and recognize that your energy, your well-being, and your joy are sacred.

Because they are.

In the pages ahead, you'll learn to

- design rituals that fuel every dimension of your life,
- reclaim your energy as your most precious asset,
- protect your attention and inner world with conscious boundaries,
- navigate resistance without abandoning yourself.

These aren't just frameworks, they're invitations to stop merely surviving your days and start living them with intention and grace.

CHAPTER 5

Harnessing the Power of Rituals

Rituals are the doorway to creativity. They give form to what might otherwise be formless. They structure the time and space of our days.

Julia Cameron, *The Artist's Way*

We've been conditioned to view productivity as a race—to do more, achieve more, control more, all in less time. But real productivity—the kind that fuels sustainable success without sacrificing soul—has never been about speed. It's about depth, choosing presence over performance, intention over inertia.

In this chapter, you'll challenge everything you've been told about busyness and success. You'll learn to shift from rigid, depleting routines to intentional, life-affirming rituals. Not to manage time better, but to align your time with your true priorities, and in doing so, to feel deeply, vibrantly alive.

Rituals vs Routines: A Life Nourished, Not Depleted

At first glance, routines and rituals may appear identical: both involve structure, repetition, and action. But what separates them isn't how they look from the outside—it's how they feel on the inside and what they cultivate over time.

Rituals aren't elaborate ceremonies saved for special occasions. Rituals nourish your nervous system and reconnect you to meaning—not just motion—so you don't lose yourself in the grind, waking one day to pick up the pieces of a life that slipped away.

> *Rituals are the difference between running on empty and running with intention.*

High-performing professionals who integrate rituals into their day—during transitions, breaks, reflective practices, or meaningful connections—report higher resilience, stronger emotional intelligence, and more sustained well-being. Why? Because rituals build internal coherence. They align your time with your values. They help you feel like *yourself* inside the life you're leading. They offer that elusive sense of purpose you've been searching for—the one you may think others have mastered while you're still wondering where yours went.

Before we explore how to design your own rituals, let's pause to honor a core truth: **Not all structures are created equal.**

Routine	Ritual
Feels obligatory or draining	Feels intentional and energizing
Done on autopilot	Done with presence and awareness
Focuses on productivity or outcome	Focuses on meaning and alignment
Easily skipped or resented	Emotionally connected and self-honoring
Maintains unconscious momentum	Deepens connection and purpose
Often tied to control and proving	Grounded in care and self-trust
Something you push through or force	Something you look forward to
Can burn you out	Can bring you back to life

Rituals are the difference between running on empty and running with intention—between checking a box and charging your soul.

How Rituals Restore Your Nervous System

Rituals aren't just prettified routines, they're deeply personal interventions that bring us back to ourselves.

Unlike routines that tether us to the clock, rituals anchor us to our core. They offer not just structure but sanctuary. They remind us that we are not machines built to produce but humans meant to feel, connect, and create meaning in motion.

A ritual can take many forms, such as:

- Sitting in stillness with your coffee instead of scrolling
- Stepping outside for fresh air after a draining meeting
- Journaling with presence
- Listening to music that stirs your heart
- Preparing a meal with your partner
- Playing a board game or a sport with your child
- Sharing a moment of laughter with someone you love

These aren't trivial moves. They're micro-recalibrations for your nervous system. Research from UCLA's Mindful Awareness Research Center confirms that even brief, intentional practices of mindfulness can reduce stress, strengthen immunity, and sharpen decision-making.

When I began weaving mindful practices like these into my days—not as obligations, but as sacred choices—I noticed a profound shift. My system softened. The chaos quieted. I started to feel like myself again. And with that, a desire arose: to spend my time differently. Not to rebuild my entire life overnight, but to replace meaningless activity with actions that nourished me.

At first, it felt like an exercise in self-discipline (and I've heard—and said—all the excuses: "I don't have time for that"). But I was no longer willing to let Erica's voice of fear keep me small or from radiating from within. And so, a simple phrase rose up in me:

I Can Fit That In.

That phrase became more than a mindset, it became a compass. A shift in how I designed my life. The north star that would later become the foundation for my method, guiding thousands to realign with what matters most.

When I believed I could fit in what filled me up, I stopped treating my well-being as optional. I stopped handing over my time to urgency, anxiety, and the noise of what I couldn't control. Instead, I began honoring what I *could* shape: my attention, my actions, and my energy.

I stopped micromanaging the uncontrollable—like the weather, the moods of others, or the outcomes I once obsessed over—and started mastering what was always mine: my internal state.

That mindset changed everything. I no longer let the world hijack my peace. I no longer mistook worry for preparation or urgency for importance. I wasn't willing to suffer for what I couldn't shift.

I fit in what truly mattered: date nights, earlier wake-ups for meditation and conscious coffee brewing and sipping, earlier bedtimes, movement that restored and nourished my body, swapping mindless streaming or scrolling for reading, silencing the constant news cycle to protect my mental clarity and mood.

You can fit in what matters.

You can fit in the breath. The pause. The walk or run. The stillness. The meal. The inner work. The dance. The conversation that reconnects you. You transform how you see yourself—and, as a result, how you see the world. It becomes more vibrant and more colorful.

You can fit in what matters. And in doing so, create a life that doesn't just function, but feels like it's *yours*. A life you're proud to live. A life designed from peace, not pressure.

The Athlete's Edge: Rituals over Routines

High performers in both sports and business know that success isn't just what you do, it's how you do it. At the highest levels, performance is a mental and emotional game. If it were solely physical, practice and drills would be enough. (And in business, degrees and credentials would be enough too.) But mastery demands more: It calls for intentional rituals that anchor, focus, and align.

- Tiger Woods took a grounding breath before every tee shot, recalibrating his focus and nervous system.
- Tom Brady ritualized intention and belief over chasing perfection, tuning in to presence.
- Novak Djokovic credits meditation and breathwork with helping him manage intense emotions with grace and adaptability.

- Michael Jordan laced up a fresh pair of sneakers before every game—not for the shoes themselves, but for the ritual of centering himself in the moment.

These were not merely habits; they were practices of reverence. They honored the moment, connected mind to body, and anchored these athletes to themselves and their purpose.

Your calendar may resemble everyone else's. But your energy and intention can transform the experience. In this way, rituals become your performance strategy, not just to get through the day, but to elevate it. They cultivate presence, rhythm, and resilience in a world that rewards reactivity.

You don't need to be a world-class athlete to treat your time and energy with reverence. Start with what's already in your day—your commute, your morning routine, your work meetings—and infuse them with presence. The moment you choose to approach these ordinary spaces with intention, you begin the shift from routine to ritual.

The Ritual Loop Framework—Structure That Liberates

Many of us have leaned on structure to rise to challenges and deliver results. But over time, the very structure that once supported us can start to feel like a cage. What once empowered us can become a source of numbness. What once offered freedom can evolve into a relentless demand for perfection.

Enter the Ritual Loop Framework. This five-step process transforms draining routines into energizing, intentional rituals that align with your values and nourish your nervous system.

I'll introduce the framework now—you'll get the chance to apply it later in the realignment rituals section of the chapter.

The Five Phases of the Ritual Loop Framework

1. Awareness: What's not working?
You can't transform what you don't notice. Ask yourself,

- Which parts of my day feel heavy or disconnected?
- Where am I operating on autopilot?
- What drains my energy?

Awareness is the flashlight that reveals hidden friction.

2. Intention: What do I want this moment to mean?
Every action sends a message to your nervous system. Intention is choosing that message. Ask yourself,

- What do I want to feel during this?
- What value or purpose does it serve?

Even brushing your teeth can become a grounding ritual. A meeting can shift from a task to a moment of connection.

3. Design: How can I honor this moment?
Bring creativity and playfulness into the equation. Small shifts can transform your experience.

- A rushed scroll becomes a mindful coffee ritual.
- A dreaded workout transforms with music you love.
- A draining Zoom meeting becomes a chance to breathe deeply (if you're attending) or connect more personally (in a one-on-one meeting).

You're not just changing the activity—you're changing your relationship to it.

4. Reverence: How can I be fully present?

Reverence is the soul of ritual. It's choosing to treat the moment as sacred. No incense or sage required. (Though, if that's your thing, go for it!)

- "I'm here for this."
- "This matters enough for my full attention."

Rituals met with reverence become portals to clarity and self-trust.

5. Integration: What's shifting? What's sticking?

Rituals evolve. Check in with yourself:

- Is this still energizing me?
- Has it become autopilot again?
- What ripple effect is it creating in my energy and presence?

Integration keeps your rituals alive and nourishing long after the initial momentum fades.

Real-Life Ritual Snapshots Across Life's Dimensions

Rituals aren't confined to quiet mornings; they shape the very culture of your life, in your work, your home, and your relationships.

In the Workplace

Even in the most corporate environments, rituals can be a muted act of leadership. A senior executive I know begins meetings with five minutes of gratitude, setting the tone for presence and connection. Another leader schedules quarterly "vision walks" in nature to reflect on goals and recalibrate intentions. During my own business development days, I invited prospects and contacts to join me for "sweat-working"—workouts followed by smoothies and real conversation, deepening relationships beyond transactional interactions. These rituals created cultures of trust, well-being, and authenticity.

Your workplace rituals don't have to mirror someone else's to be meaningful. They simply need to be genuine. Whether you lead a team, manage projects, or contribute as an individual, rituals can help you feel anchored and energized, even amid pressure. Consider starting your day with a five-minute "focus reset," reviewing your top priorities and setting a clear intention before diving into emails or meetings. Or create a ritual of stepping outside for a few breaths between meetings to reset your nervous system and return with clarity.

Team rituals are equally powerful. Invite colleagues to share a "one-word check-in" at the start of meetings, create space for genuine recognition and appreciation, or schedule a regular brainstorming session away from desks or screens to cultivate fresh thinking. Even seemingly small gestures—like sending a midweek note of encouragement to your team or hosting a "virtual coffee chat" with remote colleagues—can spark connection and lift morale.

The key is to design rituals that reflect your leadership style, values, and work culture. Remember: Rituals aren't about adding more complexity to your day. They're about adding more intention. When you bring care, attention, and presence to these moments, they become anchors of resilience, focus, and connection—not just for you, but for everyone you interact with.

In Partnerships or Marriage

Creating rituals with your partner or spouse is a powerful way to preserve intimacy and connection amid the velocity of modern life. Craig and I nurture connection through simple, intentional practices—salt baths, screen-free walks, gardening, morning coffee talks, or taking out the paddleboard. These are tiny moments of choosing each other again and again. You can ritualize connection with your partner through small yet powerful moments: sharing a genuine compliment, a touch, an "I love you," or a simple "I'm grateful for you today." These rituals calm the nervous system, build emotional safety, and create a resonance between your hearts.

But you don't need to copy our rituals to experience their power. The beauty of partnership rituals lies in their uniqueness to the two of you. Maybe it's a shared Sunday morning ritual where you both set your intentions for the week. Maybe it's cooking a meal together without distractions, sharing a playlist that transports you, or reserving one night a month as a "tech-free date night" to reconnect.

The key is to design rituals that honor your rhythms, preferences, and values as a couple. They can be daily, weekly, or seasonal—whatever feels natural and sustainable. It might be as simple as sharing a morning cup of tea in silence, taking a walk at sunset, or setting aside five minutes before bed to reflect on your day. What matters is not the size or complexity of the ritual, but the *intention* behind it: to consciously connect, to hold space for each other, and to nurture the bond that often gets overshadowed by the demands of daily life.

When you approach these moments with reverence, they shift from being another task on the list to being a lifeline—a sacred container that holds your relationship steady amid the chaos.

With Children

Our family rituals have evolved as our boys have grown. What we gravitated to when they were five and six is different when they're at nine and ten. From gratitude expressions at dinner, Friday movie nights, sushi-making, playing "restaurant," rec center days with Dad, to guided meditations—each ritual whispers, "You matter. I'm here." These aren't just warm memories; they're foundational moments that teach kids how to return to themselves.

But these examples are just a glimpse of what's possible. Family rituals aren't about replicating someone else's traditions—they're about discovering what resonates with your family's unique rhythm and values. Maybe your mornings begin with a shared affirmation or a silly dance in the kitchen. Maybe your evenings include storytelling or a technology-free window of time to reconnect. The essence is to infuse moments of connection into your everyday life, to create pockets of presence that feel natural and meaningful for your family.

These rituals don't need to be perfect, scheduled, or performative. They can be as simple as a bedtime gratitude practice, an after-school snack ritual, or a Saturday morning pancake tradition. The point is to create intentional moments where your child feels seen, heard, and loved—moments where you model presence, self-care, and connection.

With Friends

Intentional rituals—whether they are forest walks, shared hobbies, or just chatting on the phone—deepen bonds and remind us of who we are beyond roles and routines. But these rituals don't have to be elaborate to matter. They might be as simple as a monthly coffee catch-up, a quarterly dinner where everyone brings a dish, or a seasonal "friend retreat" to reconnect and reflect.

The essence is to design rituals that reflect the special dynamics of your friendships—whether it's laughter over a meal, silent support on a hike, or a simple check-in text that says, "I'm thinking of you." When you ritualize connection with friends, you're not just maintaining relationships; you're enriching them with intentionality and care.

With Extended Family Members

Gatherings like family reunions, birthdays, and holiday celebrations are more than just social occasions, they're rituals that sustain generational connection. These moments give everyone a reason to pause, reconnect, and remember where they come from.

As we grow up and carve our own paths, it's easy for these connections to slip into the background, overshadowed by the demands of work, parenting, and daily life. But when we create space to gather intentionally—whether for a Sunday dinner, a weekend get-together, or a holiday tradition—we're doing more than adding an event to the calendar. We're weaving a thread of continuity that whispers, "You're part of my story, and I'm part of yours."

These rituals don't need to be extravagant—a yearly visit, a monthly check-in call, or a meal can create lasting bonds. What matters is not the scale but the intention: to gather, share, laugh, heal, and create memories that bridge the past, present, and future.

For those with strained or distant family relationships, even a small indication of care—a handwritten note, a thoughtful text, an invitation to reconnect—can be a meaningful step toward healing or reimagining connections (if that's something you choose). Rituals with extended family don't need to be perfect or elaborate, they simply need to be infused with heart.

A Life Woven from Intentionality

These examples of rituals at work, in partnerships, and with children, friends, and extended family show that rituals are not confined to a certain setting or scale. They are woven into the fabric of how we show up, how we connect, and how we live. Each ritual, no matter how small, carries the potential to shift our energy, nurture our relationships, and align our daily lives with what matters most.

The beauty of rituals is that they are deeply personal and endlessly adaptable. You are the architect of your own rhythms. Whether you choose to create a shared family meal, a morning of quiet reflection, a simple text to a friend, or a leadership practice that anchors your team, you are crafting a life not driven by default, but by design.

This is your invitation to let rituals be more than moments—they are how you express care, clarity, and connection in every dimension of your life.

From Awareness to Embodiment

By now, you've journeyed through a reorientation from the grind of autopilot routines to the possibility of intentional, soul-nourishing rituals. You've glimpsed how small shifts in how you approach your day can ripple outward, transforming not just your energy, but the quality of your presence and your impact.

Awareness is the doorway, and the rituals ahead are where intention comes to life. They're not about adding complexity to your life, they're about distilling it down to what matters most. These rituals offer you an opportunity to design your day around alignment, not obligation. To create moments of connection, clarity, and vitality, right in the midst of your existing schedule.

> *Awareness is the doorway, and the rituals ahead are where intention comes to life.*

These practices are your invitation to stop managing your day, and start leading it with purpose.

Realignment Ritual to Get Started

This section—and the similar sections at the end of each chapter in part 2—is your invitation to understand the power of rituals by living them. They aren't rigid tasks, but flexible, soulful structures that meet you where you are.

When you engage them, you'll begin to feel a shift—not just in how you manage time, but in how you embody presence, purpose, and alignment.

The goal is to cultivate a life where each action feels intentional, where energy is restored rather than depleted, and where your leadership—both personal and professional—reflects deep coherence between what you value and how you live.

Realignment Ritual: Create One Ritual Loop

Choose one area of your life that currently feels like a draining routine. Then, for the next week, apply the Ritual Loop Framework:

- **Awareness:** What feels misaligned, hollow, or depleting?
- **Intention:** What do I want this moment to foster in me?
- **Design:** How can I make it more easeful, expressive, or connected?
- **Reverence:** How can I bring full presence to it?
- **Integration:** What's shifting? What's working?

Then, reflect:

- How did this shift your energy?
- What did it change about how you showed up?
- What surprised you?

Rituals aren't just for centering your day, they're the scaffolding for something deeper: a life you can actually sustain—a life where you're not pouring from an empty cup or chasing productivity at the cost of presence. A life where alignment and vitality are not goals you aspire to, they're the natural result of how you choose to show up.

CHAPTER 6

Building a Sustainable Life

We think, mistakenly, that success is the result of the amount of time we put in at work, instead of the quality of time we put in.

Arianna Huffington

You've spent much of your life mastering time—managing calendars, optimizing schedules, executing with precision. You've likely built a career on performance, productivity, and pushing through. But if you've ever found yourself asking, *Why am I still so tired? Why does it still feel like too much?*—you're not alone.

This chapter shifts the focus from managing hours to stewarding your life force. From measuring progress by what gets done, to honoring how you feel as you do it. Energy isn't just a resource to squeeze more from, it's a vital, renewable, yet often underutilized source of power.

We've been conditioned to think of energy as purely physical, as if it's something you either have or don't based on sleep or caffeine. But your energy is multidimensional, made up of mental, emotional, physical, spiritual, and relational well-being. It's the very essence of how you show up in the world.

This next evolution of your self-leadership, fulfillment, and well-being is about sustainability. And that begins with a different kind of attention. Not to your time, but to your state. Efficiency is a byproduct of your sustainable self-leadership.

This next evolution of your self-leadership, fulfillment, and well-being is about sustainability.

You've already come a long way, not just in these pages, but in the quiet recalibrations already unfolding in your life. You've started to name what matters. You've begun to feel where your energy rises and where it leaks. You've remembered that your spark is worth protecting.

Now comes the real turning point: How do you build a life that sustains your spark?

Time Management Is Not the Same as Energy Stewardship

We've established you don't need another app, planner, or system to squeeze more into your day. What you need is a new operating system—one built on energy, not obligation.

No matter how much you achieve or attain, if your mind is still racing and your spirit remains tired, it's time to ask a deeper question:

Am I managing my energy, or simply trying to outrun my depletion?

Energy determines how you show up, how deeply you connect, how consistently you perform, and how fully you lead. Unlike time, energy can be replenished—if you understand what fuels it and what drains it. Time is finite. Energy is renewable.

As Sadhguru reminds us in *Inner Engineering*, the goal isn't to escape gravity by doing more—the goal is to access grace by becoming lighter, more expansive, more present. Rituals help us make that leap—by changing how we approach life's demands, not by removing them.

The word *ritual* comes from the Latin root *ritus*, meaning "the proven way"—a reminder that rituals are not arbitrary, but intentional practices that ground us in what works. Meanwhile, the word *spirit*—and *respiration*—derive from the Latin *spiritus*, meaning "breath." When we engage in rituals, we're not merely performing an action. We are, quite literally, breathing life into our existence. Each ritual becomes an act of conscious presence, a way of choosing not just what gets done, but how we *are* as we do it.

You've learned to manage your time. Now, you're ready to steward your energy.

Think of it like tending a fire. Time is the wood, but energy is the flame. You can stack as much wood as you like, but if the fire's not tended, it burns out—or worse, smolders into smoke and ash. The shift is learning how to keep the flame alive—not by adding more fuel, but by feeding it with intention, breath, and presence.

You Can't Add What Nourishes Until You Subtract What Drains

Most high achievers try to fix burnout by adding more productivity hacks or coping strategies. This is where the influencer world has made it especially tricky. You see someone touting a "life-changing" routine—buy the products, follow the routine, and wait for the magic to click. You stuff it into your already packed day, hoping this one will finally make the difference. Yet, deep down, you fear it's just another fleeting trend, another Band-Aid for the real issue.

The hard truth is that real sustainability doesn't begin with addition. It begins with subtraction. You must first cut out what drains you.

Energy leaks often hide in plain sight: autopilot routines, outdated roles, mismatched expectations, and unspoken stories of obligation. These aren't small annoyances; they're slow weakenings of your vitality, clarity, and capacity to live with purpose.

A former client—a partner at a global consulting firm—came to me utterly exhausted. Not from the sheer hours she worked, but from the invisible performance she maintained: saying yes when she meant no, micromanaging instead of trusting, attending dinners she didn't have energy for. Her fear? If she didn't do it all, she'd lose credibility.

But in trying to be indispensable to others, she had become invisible to herself.

Together, we began subtracting. One draining meeting declined, another postponed. A late-night email left unanswered until tomorrow. The cluttered bonus room cleared to make space for the art studio she longed for. The stack of five books on her nightstand reduced to one. One committee role paused. Her name removed from the volunteer lunch duty list at her children's school. And then another.

With each subtraction, her energy didn't just return, it expanded.

"For the first time in years," she told me, "I feel like I'm living my life, not just trying to get through it."

Let's name the most common energy drains:

- **Chronic overcommitment**: Saying yes because you can, or because you're afraid to disappoint.
- **Unclear boundaries**: Letting others dictate your time and energy.
- **Toxic positivity or relationships**: Forcing a smile when what you need is space and authenticity.
- **Digital overload**: Consuming more than you create, scrolling as a substitute for soul-nourishing engagement.
- **Inner criticism**: The voice that depletes you faster than any overflowing inbox ever could.

Energetic integrity is choosing, over and over, to stop feeding what no longer feeds you.

Designing Micro, Macro, and Transitional Energy Rituals

Energy is not a one-size-fits-all equation. It rises and falls throughout the day and is shaped by your environment, relationships, focus, and physiology. To sustain vitality—not just for a quarter or a season, but over the arc of your life—you must design rituals that meet your energy where it is and guide it where you need it to go.

This is where ritual becomes both medicine and momentum.

To make this personal and practical, let's explore three dimensions of rituals: micro, macro, and transitional.

Micro Rituals

Micro rituals are brief, repeatable practices that ground your nervous system and return you to presence, without adding to your to-do list. You can refer to the practices that resonated most with you from part 1 or others you've discovered along the way.

Examples of micro rituals include the following:

- A three-minute breathing ritual between meetings
- A moment of visualization before your first Zoom call
- Standing barefoot outside to recalibrate your energy
- A centering affirmation before opening your inbox
- A gratitude pause with morning coffee or tea

These rituals don't consume your time, they give it back to you.

Macro Rituals

Macro rituals zoom out, tethering you to the larger arc of who you are and who you're becoming. These weekly, monthly, or seasonal practices align you with your core values, vision, and purpose.

Examples of macro rituals include the following:

- A Sunday morning ritual for setting intentions
- Creative time with no agenda—writing, painting, reading, singing, dancing, reflecting
- A quarterly solo retreat in nature to reset (as simple as a day hike or beach visit)
- A walk-and-talk ritual with a partner, friend, or family member each week
- An annual rhythm of celebration or recalibration

One of my favorite macro rituals began when our boys were toddlers: Craig and I plan a sun-soaked getaway during the first week of January—a pause after the holiday rush. It's our way of celebrating the past year and looking forward to what's ahead. We intentionally place less emphasis on holiday gifts and more on this shared experience as the gift itself. This ritual reminds me: We work hard, and we're also allowed to live well, savor life, and recalibrate in a way that nourishes the soul.

Transitional Rituals

Transitions are where most of us leak energy. We rush from one role to another—meeting to parenting, laptop to dinner table—without fully arriving. Transitional rituals act as energetic buffers, helping you land and recalibrate.

Examples of transitional rituals include the following:

- Lighting a candle or playing music to mark the end of the workday
- A silent drive or walk before stepping into your home
- A breath, a stretch, or a grounding affirmation before switching tasks
- Changing clothes or washing your face to reset your internal state

One client, a marketing executive and mother of three, once told me: "Sitting in my car for five minutes before I walk in—that's the most important five minutes of my day. It helps me re-enter as the version of me my family deserves."

Even Craig, during high-stakes multi-million dollar real estate deals, would sometimes pull onto our street with his mind still entangled in crisis negotiations. One moment: commissions on the line. The next: our boys asking lighthearted questions about football players. Though he was present physically, his energy was still caught up in the deal. Later, he realized: "Two minutes of grounding myself while still in the car could have changed everything, not just for me, but for everyone in the house."

This is the quiet power of transitional rituals. They're not just about smooth handoffs, they're about honoring the space between, ensuring you don't just move through your life, but arrive in it fully.

Transformational Examples of Energy Shifts

Profound energy shifts don't require overhauls, they begin with small, intentional changes in often overlooked places.

The Environment Shapes Energy

Your physical space isn't just a backdrop, it's a silent influencer of your mental and emotional state. Visual clutter increases cognitive load, while nature-inspired elements (like plants, textures, and natural light) restore calm and enhance creativity. A 2022 Journal of Environmental Psychology study confirmed that sensory-intentional spaces elevate mood, focus, and clarity.

If you often work from home, consider this: My own office is intentionally designed for peace and inspiration. I spend hours creating, running the business, delivering virtual speaking engagements, and coaching clients here. The navy accent wall, ocean artwork, and living ZZ plant aren't random decor, they're anchors of calm and clarity. More than once, people have said, "Just seeing your Zoom background makes me feel calmer." It's more than aesthetics, it's energetic impact.

Here are some simple changes you can make:

- Move your desk near natural light.
- Add live plants or calming natural textures.
- Incorporate artwork that grounds you in your purpose.
- Design your space so it nourishes your energy before your work even begins.

Aligning Tasks with Energy Rhythms

You don't need to do everything at your best, you simply need to do the right things when you're at your best.

Chronobiology—the science of natural energy cycles—reveals that analytical thinking peaks mid-morning, while creative flow often emerges later. Daniel Pink's *When* underscores how aligning tasks with your natural rhythms boosts performance.

I reserve my sharpest mental hours for writing, coaching, and strategic thinking. Tasks like accounting, CRM updates, or inbox management are best left for late afternoon, when focused energy naturally wanes. Alignment is about honoring your body's wisdom.

Ask yourself,

- When am I most mentally clear and focused?
- When do I experience cognitive or emotional lows?
- Which tasks feel misaligned with my natural rhythm?

With this awareness, you can redesign your calendar to prioritize what matters, and fit in tasks that match your energy.

Knowing When to Pause

Not every day is designed for peak output. Some days call for a slower, more easeful approach—one infused with grace. An emotional low, disrupted sleep, or inner static isn't a flaw, it's a signal. Pushing through is like driving with a flat tire.

Consider creating a "grace list"—a menu of lower-lift tasks for days when your energy is off. Maybe that means rescheduling meetings, clearing the decks for deeper rest, or simply acknowledging your limits. The key is honesty: When you honor your actual capacity, you influence outcomes with clarity and authenticity.

Because no matter what, your energy speaks louder than your words.

Unlearning the Productivity Myth

Productivity that ignores well-being is simply polished self-abandonment.

We've been conditioned to believe that worth equals output, that slowing down is failure, and that stillness is wasted time. But the most effective leaders—the ones who create sustainable impact—don't measure success by how much they do. They measure it by how they feel while doing it.

They move toward alignment, not adrenaline rushes. They rest before depletion. They release roles, routines, and relationships that no longer serve their evolution. They get clear on what truly fits into their lives.

This is not indulgence, it's the new standard of leadership: more grace, deeper impact, and a life lived in resonance with who you are and what you value.

Leadership Impact: Energized Presence as Influence

Before a word is spoken, your presence speaks.

Have you ever noticed how a well-respected, well-liked leader walks into a room and suddenly, the atmosphere shifts? It could be in a company you worked for, an advisory board you served on, or even a community gathering. They carry a frequency—a calm, grounded coherence of someone fully embodied and aligned.

I've felt this around leaders like my friend Susie from my years in business development roles. She led with poise and grace, even amid intense pressure and personal challenges. It wasn't just her strategies or decisions that made an impact, it was her presence and I admired her.

Presence is the future of leadership. Not hustle for hustle's sake, not hyperactivity masquerading as productivity—presence, which begins with energy.

Energized Leaders Create Energized Cultures

Workplace research converges on one truth: The emotional tone of a leader sets the energetic tone of the culture. People don't leave companies, they leave bad leaders.

You are a tuning fork. When you're grounded, others calibrate to you. When you're scattered, others splinter.

> *People don't leave companies, they leave bad leaders.*

Real-world examples illustrate this:

- A CEO opens board meetings with a moment of mindful breath, setting a tone of presence and focus.
- A manager blocks creative hours instead of cramming back-to-back calls, modeling boundaries.
- A founder regulates their nervous system before giving feedback, ensuring clarity over reactivity.

These aren't productivity hacks. They're energetic commitments. They reflect a conscious choice to lead not from control, but from calm, clarity, and resilience. These leaders understand they can't control every external event, but they can always choose how they respond.

Grace is contagious. So is chaos.

The best leaders I know don't dominate with the loudest voices or the longest resumes, they lead with the cleanest energy. They create space. They speak fewer words, but each carries authenticity and resonance. They listen with full presence. When they falter, they reset rather than retreat.

They know their most powerful leadership tool isn't just their expertise or vision, it's their regulation. Their energetic presence is their legacy, and it elevates those around them.

A Client Story: From Dimmed Light to Magnetic Leadership

Cara, an executive client leading a $300M division, was a high performer, but energetically, she was running on fumes. "I don't feel like a leader," she confided. "I feel like a crisis manager, constantly putting out fires."

She wasn't burned out, she was faded out. Her days left her no space for proactive, strategic, focused work. Her influence felt diluted, and she couldn't pinpoint how she'd reached this point, much less how to reclaim her presence.

We started small—introducing simple rituals and elevating routine actions into intentional practices: breathwork before the day began, a screen-free walk mid-afternoon, nourishing lunches, and a dedicated three-hour block every Friday for focused work and personal reflection.

Within weeks, both Cara and her team noticed a palpable shift. "You seem more present," a VP told her. "You're not as rushed anymore."

As she fueled herself differently—creating space not just for others, but for herself—her sense of self blossomed. Communication improved at home, and she felt genuinely connected to her family. Her state of being had shifted because her daily strategy had to.

Her leadership deepened as her confidence was lifted, not through doing more, but by being more.

This is how energy becomes your most powerful leadership asset.

From Insight to Implementation

You've journeyed through a powerful reframe—from managing time to stewarding energy. You've seen how subtle mindful shifts can expand your capacity, sharpen your clarity, and reconnect you to what matters most.

But these insights won't truly transform your life until they're lived. Knowing isn't enough. To embody this shift—to create a life that doesn't just sustain you but energizes you—you need practices that anchor the wisdom you've gained.

The practices ahead are not an add-on to your busy life; they are a return to alignment. They're your invitation to consciously design how you show up in the world, moment by moment. They'll help you cultivate a life that supports your well-being, presence, and impact, not through force, but through daily rituals that feed your energy and spirit.

This is the work of a sustainable, intentional life. This is where transformation becomes a lived reality.

Realignment Rituals to Steward Your Energy

The realignment rituals in this chapter are intentional, restorative invitations to shift how you engage with your life, work, and inner landscape. If you want to have coworkers notice your renewed energy, you need to be like Cara and start small with these rituals.

Rooted in energy stewardship, sustainable success, and embodied presence, these practices offer a bridge from knowing to becoming. They're not rigid routines but living frameworks designed to cultivate alignment and a sense of true belonging within yourself.

Realignment Ritual: Craft Your Layered Ritual Map

Choose one ritual from each category:

- **Micro**: What two to five minute ritual can shift your energy tomorrow?
- **Macro**: What weekly or seasonal ritual could root you more deeply in your values?
- **Transitional**: What daily transition would benefit from more presence?

Write them down. Put them on your calendar. Treat them not as extras, but as essentials—non-negotiables. Rituals you won't betray or abandon, no matter how busy life gets.

Realignment Ritual: Lead with Your Frequency

Before your next conversation,

- step away from stimulation and take three slow breaths;
- ask yourself, "How do I want to be experienced right now?";
- set a silent intention—clarity, compassion, calm authority, peace;
- then, enter—not from pressure, but from presence.

Afterward, reflect:

- How did it feel to lead with presence?
- How did this shift your energy and influence the interaction?

As you close this chapter, ask yourself,

- Where am I leading from depletion, and what needs to shift?
- What is one ritual I can adopt to recharge my energy each day?
- How do I want others to feel in my presence?

This is what sustainable influence looks like. Not urgency. Not perfection. But energetic coherence—the invisible leadership quality that changes everything.

CHAPTER 7

Protecting Your Peace

You have the right to leave any story you don't find yourself in. You have the right to protect your joy, your peace, and your energy.

Maya Angelou

There comes a moment—muted but defining—when you must choose: maintain the comfort of others, or honor the clarity of yourself. This chapter is about that moment. The one where you stop mistaking being needed for being worthy. Where you choose peace over performative politeness. Where self-respect stops whispering and starts drawing bold lines.

If you're like me—and like most high achievers I work with—you've spent years, even decades, saying yes when your body or intuition said no. Agreeing to meetings you had no space for. Saying yes to the lunch you couldn't afford to give time to. Taking the call, the favor, the extra lift not because you wanted to, but because you didn't want to disappoint. You were admired and relied upon, and being needed became your unconscious metric for value.

But beneath that performance was a quieter truth: Every unnecessary yes was a slow leak of your life force. Every unspoken boundary was a subtle act of abandoning yourself.

If I had twenty dollars for each time I ignored the internal cues telling me a person, place, invite, or request wasn't right for me, I'd own a large yacht by now.

As Brené Brown writes: "Daring to set boundaries is about having the courage to love ourselves, even when we risk disappointing others."

Boundaries aren't barriers, they're bridges. They don't close us off; they return us to ourselves.

This chapter is an invitation to stand firmly and recognize that protecting your peace isn't selfish, it's sacred. Let's redefine selfishness for this modern world: Not as a tool to suppress others (as it was once weaponized against women), but as what it truly is—forcing your ideals and expecting others to live their lives according to your script.

When your energy is sovereign, your influence becomes magnetic.

Your energy is not an infinite resource. Your presence and capacity to serve others all depend on your willingness to honor that truth.

Here, you'll learn some important lessons:

- How to say no with grounded confidence—without apology or defensiveness.
- How to protect what fuels you, without abandoning your ambition or compassion.
- How to craft boundary language that's clear, calm, and emotionally intelligent.
- How to reframe boundaries not as separation, but as sovereignty.

When your energy is sovereign, your influence becomes magnetic.

The Hidden Costs of Boundaryless Living

I used to believe effort equaled worth. Especially in sales and business development, I was conditioned to be "always on." Long days, followed by industry dinners or drinks multiple nights a week. I was always performing, always adding value, always proving I deserved my seat.

And I succeeded—on the surface. Growing a corporate business within a business by 500% in just a few years didn't happen by accident; it happened because I poured my heart and soul into it. But, beneath that success was a woman slowly disappearing. I had given so much of myself away that I didn't even have the energy to enjoy the life I was building.

Cooking dinner felt like a chore. Calling a friend felt like too much. Even taking a walk or going to yoga felt like an obligation. My nervous system was frayed. My joy was a ghost.

I didn't know how to say no. I thought saying no meant I wasn't grateful or ambitious. But saying yes to everything was costing me the very life I'd worked so hard to create.

That's the hidden cost of boundaryless living: It bankrupts your joy while convincing you that you're being generous.

Boundaries aren't walls, they're filters. Living membranes that discern what's worthy of your time, attention, and energy. Without them, you absorb everything: other people's urgency, expectations, and emotional weight. Slowly, you stop recognizing your own rhythm.

Without boundaries, even the most nourishing rituals eventually collapse under the pressure of other people's needs. But with them, you return to yourself. You stop reacting and start responding from discernment, not guilt.

Saying No Clearly, Compassionately, and Powerfully

Saying no isn't selfish, it's sovereign. When spoken with clarity and care, it becomes one of the most respectful things you can offer to both yourself and others.

I once had a friend who would simply disappear—no conflict, no explanation, just silence. One day, we were close; the next, I was erased. It's a disorienting kind of grief to be ghosted by someone you love—a grief without resolution. And I wasn't alone; she had done this to others too.

It was her pattern: to disappear before discomfort, to avoid clarity under the guise of peace. But ghosting isn't grace, it's avoidance. And avoidance, no matter how polished, is not integrity.

There's always a way to honor both your boundary and someone else's humanity. You can say:

- "I care about you, but I need space right now."
- "I'm navigating something and can't show up in this relationship the way I want to."
- "I don't have the emotional capacity for this right now, and I need to honor that."

Boundaries spoken clearly and kindly create clean closure. No ghosts. No shame. Just truth. And when you're the one delivering that truth, remember that clear communication isn't cruelty, it's respect. On the receiving end, it's a reminder that not everything is about you. Time has a way of clarifying what's meant to stay and what needs to evolve—or even end.

Sometimes, you have to let things fall away, especially if they've run their course, to make space for what truly matters.

Prioritizing What Fuels You Without Guilt

If you don't prioritize your life, someone else will.

Greg McKeown

There comes a moment when the old trade-off no longer makes sense:

I am no longer available to exchange my peace for productivity.

Choosing better and discerning what's truly worthy of your time, energy, and presence, and doing so without guilt, takes effort.

For many high achievers, prioritizing yourself feels self-indulgent, or even disloyal. We've been conditioned to believe that leadership demands sacrifice and that service requires self-suppression. But, sustainable leadership demands discernment. It asks you to fuel your own fire before lighting the way for others.

In a world that rewards doing it all, saying yes to everything becomes a subtle form of self-abandonment. You end up drowning in meetings, projects, and obligations you didn't choose, but didn't resist either. Without conviction, you become reactive—at the mercy of external demands. Over time, this misalignment doesn't just lead to a breakdown; it manifests as burnout.

When Resentment Becomes the Alarm

As a corporate executive, wife, and mother, I convinced myself I could—and should—do it all. Be productive. Be polished. Be available. The pressure was relentless, but I didn't question it. I simply performed. I'd look around at others like me and think, *They've got it all together—why can't I just keep going like them?*

Until the resentment started leaking out sideways. A snippy comment here. An eye roll there. I was snapping over trivial things—like how the dishwasher was loaded or the way someone looked at me. But it wasn't about those inconsequential things. It was the slow, invisible erosion of my capacity.

And the last thing I wanted was to resemble the bad examples of leadership I'd come up through the ranks under.

One night, after yet another outburst I immediately regretted, I asked myself: *What is this really about?* The answer landed like a truth I'd long avoided:

I'm carrying too much. And I've convinced myself I have to. I've made myself a martyr.

I used to think excellence meant being endlessly available. I believed that if I didn't say yes to everything, I wasn't doing enough. But what I was really doing was performing exhaustion as proof of my value. And that way of showing up made every single thing feel like a heavy lift.

This realization was a turning point—a decision to stop outsourcing my worth and start reclaiming my power.

The Role of Guilt: A False Alarm System

Guilt will try to talk you out of your boundaries.

It whispers, *You're letting people down,* or *You're being selfish.* But guilt is often a false alarm—a reflex from your nervous system reacting to a new way of being, not your intuition signaling something's wrong.

Let's reframe those moments:

Saying no to a last-minute ask?

> Old story: *You're not being a team player.*
> New truth: **I'm honoring my priorities and can't commit right now.**

Choosing solitude over yet another networking event?

> Old story: *You'll miss out.*
> New truth: **I'm replenishing so I can lead with clarity.**

You can't be authentic without self-awareness. And you can't grow without discomfort. The key is knowing the difference between guilt and growth. While alignment can feel uncomfortable, that doesn't mean it's wrong. It means you're growing.

Guilt will try to talk you out of your boundaries.

Feel the guilt. Let it pass through like a wave—not a verdict, but a signpost. Hold the boundary. That's how you evolve.

Integrity is honoring your energy. When you do, you don't just reclaim your time, but your presence, clarity, and capacity to show up fully for what matters most.

Scripts for High-Stakes Clarity (Without Apology)

You don't owe anyone a ten-point essay on why you're honoring your capacity. Less is more; brevity is strength. Here are a few high-integrity scripts to make saying no feel clear and confident. Adapt them to your style, the person, and the context:

- "I'm focused on a few core priorities right now and can't take this on; thank you for understanding."
- "That's a meaningful opportunity, but it's not aligned with where I'm directing my energy this quarter."
- "I won't be able to join, but I'm cheering you on from here."
- "I'm practicing more intentional boundaries this season, and this doesn't fit right now."

Notice what's missing: apology, over-explanation, justification. This is about being discerning, not difficult.

When you overexplain or justify, it signals to the other person (and yourself) that you're unsure or inauthentic in your decision. It invites negotiation where there should be clarity. Their reactions might not align with your hopes because you've unintentionally conveyed that your no is negotiable.

And if you're wondering whether this is how high-level leaders operate—you're right. Most senior executives protect their mornings for uninterrupted reflection and focus. They carve out space for what matters most, and when something truly important (not just falsely urgent) arises, they adjust with intention. They own their time, align with their values, and protect their energy—just as you're learning to do now.

Every clear no you offer creates the space for a more meaningful yes.

Rituals for Sustaining Strong, Healthy Boundaries

Boundaries aren't a one-time act, they're a living rhythm. Left untended, the weeds of overcommitment, guilt, and people-pleasing creep back in.

This is where your rituals become a quiet revolution: consistent, embodied practices that rebuild your relationship with your time, energy, and self-worth.

The stronger your rituals, the steadier your boundaries.

Ritual #1. The "Pre-Yes Pause"

Before you agree to anything—a meeting, a favor, a networking event, a quick Zoom call—pause. Ask yourself,

- Am I saying yes from alignment—or from guilt, fear, or habit?
- What will this cost me energetically? What might it protect?
- If I say yes, what am I saying no to?

Ritualize this pause with a breath, a gentle hand over your heart, or a brief reflection.

Ritual #2. The Sunday Night Boundary Reset

Take fifteen minutes to look into your calendar, not just at it.

- Where is there no breathing room?
- What can you reschedule, reduce, or remove?
- What ritual can you introduce to protect your energy each day?

This isn't busywork. It's energy stewardship. It prepares you for the week ahead and keeps you from feeling frantic later.

Ritual #3. Visual Cues for Energetic Protection

Your environment shapes your state. Use visual cues to signal focus and protect your energy:

- A sign on your door: Deep Focus—Please Do Not Disturb.
- A sticky note: Does this energize me?
- Calendar blocks labeled Strategic Thinking or No External Meetings.
- A simple phrase on your laptop: I did enough today. I am enough.

A former Disney exec once shared that his CEO blocked out ninety minutes daily on his calendar with just three letters: GSD—Get Sh*t Done. It was protected time, uninterruptible except for family emergencies.

These cues create micro-boundaries for your nervous system, and macro-commitments to your leadership.

Ritual #4. Nervous System Recovery Rituals

Boundaries crumble when your nervous system is frayed. Presence is impossible in a dysregulated body. Reset daily with simple rituals:

- Breathwork after high-stress conversations
- A short, intentional walk between transitions
- Journaling to process thoughts and reclaim clarity
- Putting your phone away during family time

Rituals of regulation help your nervous system become an ally, not a saboteur. Over time, you cultivate a steady state of being that magnetizes aligned energy and deflects what no longer serves you.

Ritual #5. The Sacred No Practice

Once a week, say no to something you would've reflexively agreed to out of guilt or habit. Just one thing. Then, ask yourself,

- What did I gain?
- What did I create space for—rest, presence, clarity, joy?

Boundaries aren't burdens, they're investments. And the return is your sovereignty.

Boundaries as Leadership

Saying yes to everything dilutes your influence and erodes your leadership impact. True leadership begins with clarity—showing up fully where it matters most, because you are the CEO of your energy.

And your boundaries? They're not barricades. They're declarations of self-respect and self-mastery.

You are no longer available for resentment disguised as responsibility.

Every no to what drains you creates space for what aligns; you stop performing for others and start directing your life. You shift from reactive compliance to mindful response. You lead by example—demonstrating that authenticity is far more powerful than pretense, and that clarity is a deeper form of respect than empty words.

You are no longer available for resentment disguised as responsibility and no longer interested in applause that costs you your peace.

The Bridge Between Insight and Integration

Peace is not a theory, it's a practice. Sovereignty isn't a concept, it's a lived experience. And sustainable leadership—of yourself, your work, your relationships—begins with small, intentional acts of alignment.

The tools and rituals you're about to explore aren't checklists for "doing boundaries right." They're invitations to shift how you feel, how you show up, and how you navigate each day.

The moment you move from intellectual understanding to purposeful action, you reclaim your time, your focus, and your energy. The practices ahead will support you in that shift—helping you not only protect your peace but embody it.

Realignment Rituals to Align Your Priorities

The realignment rituals in this chapter aren't just about setting boundaries, they're about living them. While the core ideas here focus on recognizing, claiming, and communicating your boundaries, these practices are designed to help you embody those principles until they become second nature.

With intention, these rituals shift you from reactive to responsive, from drained to discerning, and from boundaryless to boldly anchored.

Realignment Ritual: The Energy Audit

Reflect and write,

- What energizes me?
- What drains me?
- What am I still doing that no longer feels aligned?
- What am I not doing that my body, mind, or spirit craves?

Then, ask,

What's one small drain I can release this week to reclaim my energy?

You can't build a sustainable life on depletion. First, release. Then, protect. Finally, devote yourself to what makes you vibrantly alive.

Realignment Ritual: Reclaiming a Misaligned Yes

This week, try this:

- **Audit your commitments.** Look at your calendar: Which meetings or tasks energize you? Which ones drain you?
- **Name one misaligned yes.** Ask: *What would I reclaim by saying no to this? If I honor this no, what will I give my time and energy to instead?*
- **Practice your reframe.** Choose a script—or craft your own—and say it aloud. Ground yourself in the truth that honoring your capacity is an act of leadership.
- **Make the move.** Send the email. Make the call. Set the boundary. Not with apology, but with self-respect. Then, pause, breathe, and let that aligned decision nourish you.

Boundaries don't diminish your impact, they refine it. They ensure that when you say yes, it's powerful, present, and purposeful.

That's the kind of leadership the world needs more of.

CHAPTER 8

Navigating Resistance with Grace and Grit

Resistance is insidious. It will assume any form, if that's what it takes to deceive you. It will never stop. Resistance will tell you anything to keep you from doing your work. It will perjure, fabricate; it will seduce. Resistance is always lying.

Steven Pressfield, *The War of Art*

You can have the best rituals, the clearest vision, and the strongest intentions, and still feel like everything just got harder. That's not a problem. That's not failure. That's resistance.

Resistance isn't a barrier on your path. It is the sign that you're on the path.

It shows up precisely when you're on the edge of transformation—when you begin shedding an outdated identity, ritualizing a new rhythm, or prioritizing your peace in a world hooked on your performance. Resistance isn't there to stop you. It's there to test your resolve. It's asking: *Will you choose alignment, or retreat to autopilot?*

This chapter is for those moments—when the rituals feel shaky, when the old voices get louder, when you wonder if all your efforts have been worth it. Here, you'll learn to spot resistance for what it truly is: a signal of growth, not a sign of failure. You'll discover tools to adapt your rituals with grace, move through internal pushback with power, and stay grounded when life pulls you off course.

Mastery isn't about never faltering—trust me, everyone does. You just need to keep returning to the self you're becoming.

Resistance Is Not the Enemy—It's the Echo of Your Evolution

If everything feels harder right now, you're not regressing, you're breaking through. Trust yourself. Trust the unseen forces of transformation.

Just as sore muscles signal growth after a tough workout, resistance appears when you're expanding beyond what's familiar. Neuroscience offers a clue: the brain's default mode network (DMN) naturally resists new habits—not because they're wrong, but because they're unfamiliar. This network hums quietly in the background, replaying old stories and clinging to well-worn thought loops. Even when those patterns drain you, the DMN prefers familiarity.

This resistance isn't personal, it's biological. Your brain is wired to favor the familiar, even if it's exhausting you.

> *But you're not here to shrink. You're here to stretch.*

As Steven Pressfield describes, resistance is a shape-shifting saboteur. It will seduce, guilt, and rationalize to stop your evolution. It whispers every reason to quit, wait, procrastinate, or shrink.

But you're not here to shrink. You're here to stretch.

One client—a managing partner at a law firm—once confided, "I used to call it procrastination. Now I realize it was fear of the unknown disguised as busywork." His ritualized time for deep, strategic thinking always got postponed—until he named the resistance. He realized he wasn't lazy; he was scared of what he might discover if he slowed down.

The good news? You can silence this resistance with simple practices you've already begun incorporating into your life—meditation, mindful breathing, intentional pauses, movement. These rituals create a space between you and the old mental loops, offering your mind room to explore new connections and possibilities.

So, when resistance arises, ask yourself,

- What is this resistance protecting?
- What belief is keeping me tethered to the familiar?
- What's the smallest next step I can take with grace?

Resistance may seem more like a wall than a window, but in truth, it's a mirror—reflecting your next breakthrough.

Evolving With Your Rituals

Rituals are not static. They are living, breathing expressions of your truth. As dynamic as you are, what once anchored you may now feel stale; not because the ritual failed, but because you've grown.

NBA player LeBron James (my youngest son's favorite) famously invests over $1.5 million a year in personal care—trainers, recovery therapies, and inflammation reduction—because the rituals that sustained him in his twenties wouldn't suffice in his late thirties. He speaks candidly about the non-negotiables that keep him sharp: days off for mental recovery, limited screen time, and quality sleep. His self-care has evolved intentionally, reflecting the shifts in his life's demands and his body's changing needs.

Adaptation doesn't mean giving up on your rituals. It means listening deeply to who you are now, honoring the evolution of your needs, and adjusting your practices to stay in alignment.

When Rituals Falter—And What to Do

Even the most soul-aligned rituals will wobble. Life gets chaotic—travel derails, sickness strikes, deadlines loom. Energy dips, the spark fades. This is feedback, not failure. What matters most is how you respond.

I've seen it time and again with clients (and in my own experience), especially with meditation. Well-intentioned professionals long to create a meditation ritual, yet without structure or accountability, it tacitly slips away. And often, it's because of the perfection mindset: Meditation must look a certain way—at dawn, for twenty minutes, delivering instant serenity. But that rigidity turns meditation into a chore, a box to check off, rather than a nourishing practice for the soul. It makes it unattainable and erodes the very peace it's meant to cultivate.

The truth is, meditation—like any ritual—isn't about performance, but anchoring into a moment of connection, even if it's messy, even if it's brief. The most sustainable rituals are those infused with grace, not pressure.

So, how do you actually stick with a ritual? Start by shifting your perspective: See it as a way to nourish your energy, nurture your spirit, and tend to your inner world. Where else in your life do you truly make space for that? Chances are, you don't, and that's exactly why rituals matter so much. When you begin to view them this way, you'll crave them. Because deep down, you know that to sustain yourself, you have to give something back to yourself.

This isn't about creating a ritual that survives chaos, rather, it's about creating a ritual that serves you even in the chaos.

You can also consider inviting accountability—with a friend, a partner, or even your child. Leave a simple note in your journal or a recurring reminder in your calendar, marking each day you practiced, no matter how imperfectly. Instead of seeing these as requirements, let them become signs of self-care as natural as drinking water or moving your body. Not because you "should," but because they make you feel more connected, more grounded, more you.

This isn't about creating a ritual that survives chaos, rather, it's about creating a ritual that serves you even in the chaos.

Common Pitfalls of Establishing Lasting Rituals

Pitfall #1: The Perfection Trap

You miss a day ... then two ... and suddenly, the ritual feels abandoned. The old story resurfaces: *If it's not perfect, it's not worth it.*

Mindset shift: Progress lives in the rhythm, not the rigidity. Rituals flex with life. One breath, one line, one pause—that's enough. Small acts, consistently chosen, are what anchor transformation.

Pitfall #2: Ritual Becomes Routine

The ritual starts to feel hollow. It's no longer giving you the energy, clarity, or groundedness it once did. You're going through the motions, checking boxes without presence.

Mindset shift: Reconnect with your *why*. Ask yourself what this ritual once gave you and how it can evolve to meet your current season. Remember: Rituals thrive on intention, not repetition. A practice that once empowered you can be reimagined into something fresh, alive, and aligned.

Pitfall #3: Cognitive Resistance ("I don't have time")

The classic excuse—life is too busy. But often, this masks a deeper resistance: the fear of making space for what truly matters.

Mindset shift: Shrink the ritual. Identify your "minimum viable ritual"—something you can do anywhere, anytime. A few deep breaths. A silent intention of affirmation. A brief check-in on your feelings. Ritual is about connection, not duration.

Pitfall #4: Emotional Resistance

You start a ritual—breathwork, journaling, movement—and suddenly, grief, anger, or anxiety surfaces. As you engage your true self and listen inward more intently, long-dormant emotions can rise. This isn't failure, it's healing. But it feels overwhelming, so you pull away.

Mindset shift: Let it move through you. Emotion surfacing isn't regression; it's release. Your ritual is doing its work—clearing what's been stuck. Greet the feelings, breathe through them, and honor the process. This is the heart of true transformation.

Pitfall #5: Behavioral Resistance ("I forgot again")

Rituals slip when they're not anchored. Life gets busy, old habits resurface, and the mind defaults to comfort. The familiar excuse emerges: *I'll do it tomorrow.*

Mindset shift: Make it visible. Use cues—a sticky note, a calendar block, an accountability buddy. Make the ritual easy to remember and rewarding to repeat. Your power isn't in *later*—it's in the **now**.

From Erin's Journey: The Lesson I Had to Relearn

Even with the best intentions and the deepest understanding of the power of rituals, I still veered off course.

While writing this book, there were grueling days and relentless deadlines. I hit walls—resisting breaks, convincing myself that stepping away would shatter the "flow" I was in. I slipped back into old patterns—pushing harder, performing, ignoring my body's quiet but persistent signals.

And the irony? I was writing about rituals. About energy. About presence. Yet, there I was, in the very struggle of cognitive and behavioral resistance I know so well. It's humbling how even with knowledge and practice, our ancient brains pull us back toward familiar patterns—reminding us that resistance is part of the process.

Craig called me on it. He knows the difference between me with and without my rituals—when I'm fueled from within versus when I'm depleted. It's visible in how I look, carry myself, communicate, and, most of all, the energy I bring.

So, I paused. I walked. I breathed. I journaled. I returned—not just to the page, but to myself.

A ritual isn't a reward for productivity, nor is it a checkbox on a to-do list. It's a living recalibration—a conscious return to the core of who we are.

Rituals for Resilience, Flexibility, and Adaptability

Rituals are living practices meant to stretch with you, not snap under pressure. High achievers often fall into the trap of believing that for a ritual to "count," it must be perfectly replicated every day. But that mindset transforms what should be a restorative practice into a rigid, self-imposed cage. True resilience doesn't come from perfection; it emerges from elasticity: your ability to adapt, bend, and stay centered as life inevitably shifts.

This is about design, not just discipline. The question becomes: How well do your rituals hold you—especially when the ground beneath you moves?

Think of your rituals like yoga poses. The structure matters, but what matters more is how the pose feels in your body today. Some days, you stretch deeply. Other days, you hold a gentler version. Either way, you show up. You return to yourself.

One of my executive clients—let's call him Alex—once anchored his mornings in a sixty-minute ritual: a workout, a cold plunge, and time for reflection or reading. Then, he became a new father. The spacious mornings he'd carved out disappeared overnight. At first, he tried to force the old rhythm, but frustration quickly replaced fulfillment.

Eventually, he shifted. He let his ritual flex rather than fracture. Some mornings, it was just twenty push-ups, a silent moment holding his daughter, and a single breath to set an intention. Workouts moved to evenings or weekends. Some days, a family walk replaced the gym altogether. He didn't abandon his ritual, he evolved it. The form changed, but the essence—presence, grounding, and vitality—remained intact.

That's ritual elasticity: honoring the core intention, even when the outward form flexes. When you practice this kind of adaptability, you're not just maintaining rituals, you're expanding your resilience. You're learning to meet yourself where you are and to carry your intentions forward, no matter how life unfolds.

Resilience Is a Rhythm, Not a Reaction

We often think of resilience as something we summon in moments of crisis. But true resilience isn't forged in the fire, it's built in the quiet, consistent return to center. The most unshakeable leaders cultivate resilience not in the moment of collapse, but in the daily rhythm of returning to themselves.

Serena Williams didn't save her breathwork and recovery practices for championship days. She ritualized them in the unseen hours, when no one was watching. These practices became her foundation—carrying her through both upsets and triumphs, allowing her to perform with grace and strength no matter the circumstances.

Howard Schultz, former CEO of Starbucks, began each day with a ritual: walking his dog in silence, preparing his mind for the day's demands. This non-negotiable created a steady inner compass. No matter the challenges he faced, he knew he could return to himself on his morning walk to retain his ability to lead with clarity.

Resilience isn't luck, it's a rhythm. It's not something you force or fabricate. It's the practice of returning to presence again and again. From that grounded state, you bounce back—you know how to reconnect with your core.

Your rituals aren't just habits. They're the invisible threads that weave resilience into your life, strengthening your capacity to rise and respond with grace.

From Perfectionism to Progression

Perfectionism rarely begets perfection, or satisfaction—only disappointment.

Ryan Holiday

Perfectionism is a master of disguise. It cloaks itself as ambition, responsibility, and high standards. But at its core, it has to do with self-protection, not excellence. It whispers that if it's not flawless, it's not worth doing. That if you can't do it perfectly, you shouldn't do it at all.

Here's what you need to hear: Perfectionism doesn't protect you. It paralyzes you.

I once coached a Fortune 100 leader who had everything lined up to launch a major initiative—budget, approvals, support. Yet, nothing moved. When I asked why, he finally admitted, "It's not ready."

But it wasn't readiness he was waiting for—it was reassurance. He feared criticism more than he valued momentum.

So, I asked him, "What if your team doesn't need perfection? What if they need to see you lead with conviction, even knowing it will evolve?"

That question landed. He launched version 1.0 with exactly that message. Was it flawless? No. But it was real. And because it was real, it was approachable and people were willing to dive in to make it better. The launch—and the vulnerability in leading without perfection—invited participation and built trust. Sometimes, done really is better than perfect.

In planning my own business, I faced this same paralysis. I would catch myself hesitating, waiting to craft the "perfect" plan, the "perfect" offer. But then, I reminded myself: If what I create and offer comes from a place of soul, authenticity, and originality, it will find its place. It will resonate.

> *Perfection feeds your ego. Progress feeds your soul.*

That's why I rarely studied how others in similar fields do things—I trusted myself, my vision, and the guidance that whispered, **Just begin.**

Perfection isn't the goal. Progress is. Perfection feeds your ego. Progress feeds your soul.

You Can't Iterate On What You Don't Start

Progress requires motion. You don't think your way into clarity—you act your way into it. Overthinking doesn't prepare you; it paralyzes you. It sends you into a holding pattern, stalling your own growth.

Rituals teach you presence, clarity, and consistency, not perfection. They cultivate trust over performance. Every time you show up for your ritual—imperfect as it may be—you're telling yourself, "I'm worthy of this moment, even as I grow."

Writing this book tested every perfectionist impulse I've had. I'd revise a single paragraph ten times, striving for that elusive "just right." But I discovered that resonance doesn't come from polish, it comes from presence.

The words that landed most deeply were the ones I wrote from my heart, not the ones I thought were perfect. When I gave myself permission to write from lived experience and spiritual connection, the message flowed—and it felt undeniably true.

So, if you're waiting for the perfect plan, flawless execution, or ideal timing—stop waiting.

Stop forcing. Start being. Be messy. There's no right way or perfect place to start. Go with what feels aligned for you and trust that's enough.

In the words of Zig Ziglar, You don't have to be great to get started. You just have to get started to be great.

From Insight to Action

Everything you've absorbed in this chapter has illuminated a vital truth: Resistance isn't an obstacle to overcome, it's a signal of evolution. It's the voice at the edge of your comfort zone, urging you to choose presence over perfection, progress over paralysis.

But insight alone isn't enough. Transformation lives in what you choose to do next.

The practices ahead are not just exercises, they're how you metabolize resistance, how you adapt your rituals with intention, and how you stretch without breaking. These practices aren't about adding more to your plate; they're about deepening your relationship with what sustains you. They're the gentle nudges that move you from reaction to resilience, from autopilot to alignment.

You don't build resilience by waiting for life to settle. You build it by showing up, again and again, with clarity and compassion, even in the midst of chaos. These practices are your gateway—not to perfect performance, but to a lived, embodied experience of grace and grit.

Realignment Rituals for Lasting Impact

As you conclude this chapter on navigating resistance with grace and grit, these practices invite you to go deeper—not just into the rituals you've built, but into the energy that fuels them. It's easy to fall into rigidity, clinging to fixed routines or mistaking structure for strength. But as we saw in Alex's story when he needed to adapt to becoming a new father, true resilience is found in adaptability.

These practices are here to help you assess how fluidly your rituals meet your evolving needs, and how consciously you're stewarding your most precious resource: your energy. By tracking your natural rhythms and evaluating the flexibility of your rituals, you'll shift from autopilot to intentionality. By writing out a clear growth statement, you create for yourself a mantra that can carry you through your most difficult challenges.

These rituals are not about adding more. They're about refining your relationship with what sustains you. They're about creating a life that's not only well structured, but vibrantly, unmistakably alive.

Realignment Ritual: Energy Mapping & Ritual Flex Test

For the next week, use a journal or a note-taking app on your phone to track your energy in three-hour increments:

- When did you feel most alive, alert, and clear?
- When were you sluggish, distracted, or irritable?
- What activities restored you? What quietly drained you?

Then, ask yourself,

- What patterns are emerging?
- How can I realign my tasks with my natural energy flow?
- What simple energy rituals can I fit in at key transition points of my day?

Let your energy—not the clock—become your compass. It's the most honest metric you have.

The ritual flex test can be done after a week of mapping your energy levels. It is meant to help you further reflect on the effectiveness of your current rituals:

- Do I measure my rituals by how perfectly they're performed, or by how deeply they serve me?
- Are my rituals designed for who I am today, or for an outdated version of myself?
- Are they tied to a fixed schedule, or to a feeling I want to sustain?
- When my rhythm is disrupted, do I feel lost, or adaptable?

If any answers reveal rigidity, that's not failure, it's feedback. Shift accordingly. Your rituals aren't meant to impress anyone. They're meant to sustain you.

Realignment Ritual: Create Your Growth Statement

Take a few minutes to reflect and write:

- **I am** ... (the self you are becoming)
- **I value** ... (what you will protect and prioritize)
- **I release** ... (what no longer serves your highest self)
- **I choose** ... (the energy, actions, and rituals you will embody)

Example:
"I am an intentional, grounded {leader, mother, father, partner, son, daughter, etc.} who creates with clarity and grace. I value peace, depth, and truth. I release the need to perform for approval. I choose rituals that nourish me and align with the life I want to live."

Speak these words aloud. Let them become your guiding star, your calibration, your silent yet powerful commitment to yourself.

PART 3

LIVING WITH CLARITY, INTENTION, AND IMPACT

Discernment in Motion

Your time is limited, so don't waste it living someone else's life. Don't be trapped by dogma - which is living with the results of other people's thinking. Don't let the noise of other's opinions drown out your own inner voice. And most important, have the courage to follow your heart and intuition. They somehow already know what you truly want to become. Everything else is secondary.

Steve Jobs

You've journeyed deep into the architecture of transformation. Now, you're ready to expand outward.

In part 1, you awakened from autopilot. You confronted outdated beliefs, reclaimed your energy, and reconnected with the truth of what fuels you. You laid the essential foundation—one of self-awareness, presence, and sovereignty.

In part 2, you built upon that foundation. You transformed draining routines into energizing rituals, designed your days with intention, and cultivated resilience in the face of resistance. You discovered that sustainable growth isn't about doing more, but living more intentionally.

The inner work of parts 1 and 2 wasn't just preparation for a more fulfilling life. It was training for a deeper form of leadership—the kind that doesn't just manage circumstances but shapes them. The kind that leads not by force, but with magnetic clarity and grounded grace.

This next part of your journey is about expansion. Bringing your inner transformation into every aspect of your life—your leadership, your relationships, and the culture you cultivate. Here, the personal becomes universal. Your rituals, reflections, and resilience are no longer just practices; they become your way of being, radiating outward and influencing the world around you.

There comes a moment in every transformational journey when the inner work—the mindset shifts, the energy realignment, the rituals—begins to shape how you show up externally. This is that moment.

I've seen this in my own journey. The more clear and aligned I became, the more I could discern where my energy was truly welcomed, and where it wasn't. Not all opportunities, not all money, are good energy exchanges. Money is simply an exchange of energy, and I was no longer willing to deplete myself just to please others for a potential payout that wasn't in alignment with who I was becoming.

I remember an opportunity early in my business—a keynote invitation for a major conference. Initially, the conversations were engaging, and I felt aligned with the people involved. But during a follow-up virtual meeting before confirmation of booking the event, a new person who would be in charge was introduced. Their energy was scattered, passive-aggressive, and it brought me right back to the corporate dynamics I'd experienced during my years on Wall Street. I felt my body tense: shoulders raised, breath shallow, jaw clenched.

After the call, I meditated and reflected. Even though it was a lucrative opportunity, I declined—gracefully but with conviction.

The timing and the energy weren't right. I knew that saying yes for the money would come at the expense of my well-being.

Two years later, the same organization reached out. The disruptive person was no longer involved, and the energy was clear, collaborative, and aligned. I accepted the invitation, and it became one of my favorite keynote engagements to date.

That's what clarity makes possible. It's not about chasing every opportunity, but discerning what aligns with your truth and being honest, compassionate, and unapologetic about what doesn't. Choosing what nourishes you, what sustains your spirit, and what keeps you rooted.

Transformation weaves the inner work into every decision—how you engage with clients, allocate your time, and invest your energy.

Living with clarity, intention, and impact means standing rooted in what matters most to you. Leading your life with discernment, not default; design, not drift.

In the chapters ahead, you'll extend this transformation into every dimension of your life—your work, your relationships, your influence, and your legacy.

CHAPTER 9

Sustaining a Life That Fuels You

When you take time to replenish your spirit, it allows you to serve others from the overflow. You cannot serve from an empty vessel.

Eleanor Brown

Beneath years of expectations, obligations, and performance lies an undeniable truth:

You are the architect of your life. Not your calendar. Not your company. Not your circumstances. You.

And I don't say this from a pedestal or a place of privilege. I say it as someone who's navigated intense adversity, who's lived the grind and felt the exhaustion. I say it because I've witnessed, over and over, how reclaiming agency isn't theoretical, it's tangible. It's practical. It's lifesaving.

You are the architect of your life.

Reclaiming authorship means designing a life that doesn't just get you through the day, but brings you back to life in the process.

For too long, we've mistaken productivity for worth. We've worn burnout like a badge of honor, glorified endless to-do lists, and confused performative strength for authentic power. We've convinced ourselves that exhaustion is the price of success.

But now you know that the true measure of a powerful life isn't how much you do. It's how intentionally—and authentically—you live.

This chapter will guide you to

- live your legacy through daily choices, not distant goals;
- align your career, relationships, and passions with purpose;
- lead your life, rather than react to it.

The most extraordinary leaders aren't the ones who grind the hardest. They're the ones who choose the most consciously. They're the ones who design a life they can sustain, and who understand that showing up with intention is far more powerful than showing off with performance.

This is where your rituals move from private practice to public resonance. This is where you stop waiting for permission and start living as the leader of your life.

Self-leadership isn't optional—it's the prerequisite for any lasting impact. If you're committed to leading yourself well, there's no limit to how far you can go.

Living Your Legacy Through Daily Choices

Legacy is not what you leave for people,
it's what you leave in them.

Parker J. Palmer, *Let Your Life Speak*

Legacy isn't a distant future etched into stone after you're gone. It's etched into the people you meet, the spaces you inhabit, the moments you shape—every single day.

It lives in your presence: in how you greet the barista, how you listen to your colleagues, how you guide your children, how you show up for hard conversations, how you navigate ordinary mornings, and how you hold space in quiet nights. Legacy isn't measured by what you build, it's measured by what you embody.

Howard Schultz understood this. Raised in public housing, he witnessed his father's job loss and the indignity that followed. That memory shaped not just his leadership at Starbucks but his values. He built a culture where part-time employees had healthcare, where stores were designed as spaces of dignity and belonging.

But his true impact wasn't the policies. It was his presence—steady eye contact, remembering names, intentional kindness. That was his legacy—soul over status.

Or look at Satya Nadella at Microsoft. When he became CEO, he didn't lead with mandates, he led with humility and empathy. He began meetings by asking, "What matters most to you right now?" That single question rewired the company's culture—from know-it-all to learn-it-all. Microsoft's market value tripled, but Nadella's real impact was how people felt working there—valued, trusted, and whole.

I've had executives from Microsoft engage in my private coaching cohort, and every one of them said the guidance and tools added something profound to what they'd already learned inside Microsoft. They realized their greatest leadership power wasn't their strategy—it was the energy they brought to every interaction.

And that kind of legacy? It's not reserved for CEOs or big names. It's available to you. Right now.

Seriously—make it about you. Stop caring so much about what others think (and you'll find you make fewer judgments about others too).

You don't need a corporate title to lead a life that matters. You just need to care more about how you live than how you look while living it.

In my own family, we've created a simple ritual. After dinner, once the kitchen is clean, we sit together. One of us leads a short meditation. We read a few pages from an inspirational book. We share reflections. It only takes twenty minutes. But in those twenty minutes, my sons learn stillness, reflection, and the power of sharing their voice. Craig and I model that leading a family isn't just about managing logistics (though it feels like that sometimes). Embodying presence and cultivating self-acceptance are qualities we're imparting on our boys. Those twenty minutes aren't just part of Craig's and my legacy as parents. They're shaping our boys' legacies too.

Legacy isn't something you leave behind someday. It's something you live now.

So ask yourself,

- What energetic imprint do I leave behind in every room I enter?
- How do I want my children, my team, and my clients to feel in my presence?
- What values do I want to be remembered for—not when I'm gone, but while I'm here?

Legacy isn't something you leave behind someday. It's something you live now—through aligned actions, meaningful rituals, and the energy you bring to every encounter.

Aligning Your Career, Relationships, and Passions with Purpose

We've been conditioned to live compartmentalized lives—one self at work, another at home, a third hidden away for rare moments of reflection. But fulfillment doesn't come from fragmentation. It comes from integration.

The deeper work invites something bolder.

To unify. To bring all of who you are into everything you do. To stop splitting yourself into roles for survival, and start living as a whole, thriving being.

Authenticity is to be consistent; not just real. Alignment makes that possible. Without it, the fear-driven ego takes over, pushing you to perform, protect, and prove. But with alignment, authenticity flows effortlessly and magnetically.

Start with Your Career

In the final chapter of my corporate life—an executive role at a Fortune 150 company—everything felt different. Not because the external dynamics changed, but because I did.

The swirl of office politics, the muted toxicity of people-pleasing, the relentless push to outpace and prove—it was all still there. But it no longer owned me. I had done the inner work to release its grip. The once-relentless inner critic softened. I no longer needed to compete or prove. I needed to honor my truth. And when I did, everything shifted.

Clients I once chased appeared effortlessly. Dream partnerships unfolded through genuine conversations. What used to feel like an uphill battle became organic flow. It wasn't that I hustled harder, but I stood in integrity. I stopped performing for validation and started living from worthiness.

This is the quiet, profound power of alignment.

I was still delivering results—more than ever, in fact—but in a way that nourished me instead of depleting me. I traded performative hustle for presence. And that made all the difference.

Fulfillment didn't come from doing more. It came from aligning more deeply with what mattered.

This isn't unique to me. Whether you're in corporate leadership, entrepreneurship, public service, or creative fields, your career can become a canvas for your purpose. Yet, too many professionals stay in roles that no longer reflect who they're becoming.

They're successful by external metrics, but silently disconnected from themselves.

It's not a skill issue. It's a soul issue.

The most fulfilled professionals aren't necessarily those who leave the system or pivot drastically. They're the ones who clarify their values and redesign their work around them. Whether they shift culture from within or create something entirely new, they move from misalignment to meaning.

Now, Let's Talk About Relationships

If your career is what you do, your relationships are the ground you walk on. They're the mirror—the ecosystem that either waters your growth or quietly stunts it.

Aligned relationships don't ask you to shrink. They make space for who you are becoming.

One client—a VP in finance—shared how, after doing deep inner work for a few months, she realized her conversations with her husband were almost entirely transactional: calendars, chores, and childcare. No dreaming. No depth. When she voiced it, she feared tension. Instead, it sparked reconnection. Together, they began co-creating a new version of their relationship—one rooted in shared growth, not silent resignation. Without her intentional awareness, this realization might have come years later—or not at all.

When you begin honoring what matters most, everything changes. You become calmer, more grounded, and—perhaps most importantly—happier.

That shift transformed my marriage too. With renewed energy and presence, I communicated more clearly and compassionately, without projecting unprocessed emotions onto Craig. Of course, I still falter. I'm human. But I've built the muscle to repair quickly. To reconnect. To right my wrongs—whether with Craig or our children. To lead, even in micro-moments, not from control, but from care.

True alignment in relationships means showing up as you are, with honesty, curiosity, and care, and inviting others to do the same.

And Then, There Are Your Passions

Your passions aren't indulgences, they're indicators. They reveal what makes you feel most alive. Whether it's movement, art, music, mentoring, or building something from scratch, your passions are where your soul exhales.

They may not be your profession, and that's perfectly fine. But they are essential to your vitality, creativity, and joy.

I see it in my leadership cohorts. People arrive chasing success, and somewhere along the way, they remember what lights them up. They start painting or drawing again. Writing. Playing instruments. Gardening. Launching side businesses. Their creativity isn't frivolous—it's fuel.

I see it in Craig. His passion for golf isn't just about the game. It's sacred time. Hours of chipping, putting, practicing—not for perfection, but to be with himself, to reset. Golf is where he finds peace and progression. That's passion in its purest form.

Aligning your career, relationships, and passions doesn't require one grand gesture. It requires a thousand small ones.

Leading (Not Reacting to) Your Life

Most people are micromanaging their lives—juggling responsibilities, reacting to pressures, constantly adjusting, all while trying to appear composed. But beneath the performance often lies an unspoken question:

Am I truly steering this life—or am I just trying to keep up?

Leading your life has less to do with controlling every outcome and more to do with reclaiming agency over your choices. It's moving from reactivity to sovereignty. From survival mode to self-trust. Leadership is managing yourself through life's circumstances.

In my high-stakes corporate years, I thought relentless control would earn me respect. If I could anticipate everything, meet every need, handle every curveball—I'd prove my worth. But what I called leadership was really conformity to outdated definitions of success, to external expectations I never truly agreed to, to a life that wasn't mine.

I didn't crash, I eroded. Silently. My energy slowly vanished, and my joy evaporated. Even simple pleasures felt heavy. The hardest truth? I wasn't just exhausted; I was disappointed in myself for surrendering the reins of my own life.

Like we discussed in the introduction, I'll never forget the night in 2017 when I sat on the couch and asked Craig, "Why do we do this? Where's the meaning in any of it?" That moment was a tiny revolution in my being. I realized I no longer wanted to chase a life that looked good from the outside. I wanted a life that felt good from the inside.

That's when I stopped performing and began leading again.

Self-leadership begins with different, quiet questions:

- Does this version of my life reflect the real me—or who I thought I had to be?
- Where am I still outsourcing my power to people, patterns, or praise?
- What decision am I avoiding because it would require me to grow?

You don't need a massive change to reclaim your life—you need a conscious choice. Just one truthful act: start with your mornings, your communication, or your boundaries. Lead with intention instead of obligation.

Yes, self-leadership can feel lonely at first. People may question your shifts or feel unsettled by your clarity. Let them. When you stop betraying yourself to stay agreeable, you become magnetic.

I've seen this most acutely as a business owner. The times I said yes out of fear or scarcity, I paid with my well-being. I recall agreeing to facilitate a virtual workshop during the pandemic for a corporate client. The red flags were there: dismissiveness, insecurities, passive-aggressive attitudes. I ignored them and still said yes. It unfolded exactly as I'd feared—disconnected and draining. I left feeling inauthentic and depleted.

And then there was the potential client who called keynote speakers "inauthentic performers" moments before inviting me to speak at their event. I could have tried to win them over. But I stood in my truth: **I don't perform—I embody.** I declined. That decision didn't just protect my peace—it clarified my path.

Ask yourself,

- What have I been tolerating that no longer reflects who I am?
- Where do I need to reclaim agency in my life?
- If I led my life like it truly mattered—because it does—what would I do differently this week?

The Mirror Within: Rewriting a Story of Resistance

Karrie walked into her office every day convinced everyone hated her. It wasn't fleeting—it was the lens through which she saw her entire professional world. Emails were sharp. Her voice, edgy. Even the CEO sometimes felt her sting. She over-performed, micromanaged, and pushed, not out of dedication, but desperation.

But as we worked together, she realized it wasn't her workplace creating the toxicity—it was the conditions she'd let her soul live within. Slowly, she began to unravel the hurt. She became honest about her inputs—news, social media, TV, stress-eating—and how much of it fueled her anxiety.

She started small: journaling in the mornings, mindful walks, creating space for stillness. Through meditation, she noticed her thoughts and finally questioned them. She reframed her narratives with compassion. She set boundaries and prioritized her presence with family. She began carving out space to meal prep for the week on Sundays.

Her most profound shift came when she recognized that her labeling her colleague as "inauthentic" was a mirror of her own inauthenticity. She saw how her need for control, defensiveness, and performance were projections of her inner turmoil.

This cracked her open. She softened. Her presence shifted. Her energy no longer drained the room, it invited openness.

Karrie's transformation wasn't a dramatic restructuring, it was a practice. A steady shift from reaction to intention. From control to clarity. From depletion to alignment.

You're not here to keep up. You're here to lead. Not by force, but by choosing alignment, again and again.

You don't need a breakdown to change direction. You don't need permission to make your life more meaningful. You don't even need certainty.

You just need to decide.

When you choose to lead your life, everything shifts. Your presence grounds. Your words resonate. Your actions ripple outward.

This is where leadership evolves beyond personal transformation—it becomes a force of elevation. You don't need to empower others—they'll feel it through your way of being.

You've done the inner work. Now, it's time to become the beacon.

CHAPTER 10

Externalizing Empowerment

Success is peace of mind which is a direct result of self-satisfaction in knowing you did your best to become the best you are capable of becoming.

John Wooden

By now, you've felt it: The rituals you once adopted for your well-being have become something more. They've begun to shape not just your inner world, but the energy you bring into every environment—office, boardroom, living room, or virtual space. You're no longer operating from exhaustion or proving. You're leading from alignment.

This chapter is about what happens next—when the life you've been designing begins to inspire others to do the same. Not through persuasion, but through presence. When your rituals move from private practice to public impact. When your clarity becomes contagious.

You don't need to lead a team to be a leader. You lead by how you live. You lead by what you model.

Modeling Rituals in a Culture of Overdrive

In today's culture of constant output, glorified overwork, and undervalued restoration, "How are you?" is often answered with a badge of busyness. It's an unconscious invitation for others to admire your importance or commiserate. But behind that badge is a subtle erosion—a sign of disconnection from self-leadership.

True leadership doesn't come from depletion. It comes from discernment—from knowing what to energize and what to release.

In a world that equates success with busyness, ritual is a quiet revolution. Harvard Business Review reports that leaders who engage in daily mindfulness practices experience a 31% increase in resilience and 25% greater clarity in decision-making. This isn't just about reducing stress, but restoring the system that holds it.

Rituals don't merely regulate your nervous system, they calibrate your influence. They create a ripple effect.

And they don't need to be grandiose to be powerful. As you've seen in part 2, rituals include the micro-moves that rewire what leadership looks like—from reactive to rooted.

In my own experience, there were mornings when I felt the pull of competing priorities: guilt for leaving Craig to manage the kids while I went for a run or to yoga, or the inner voice whispering that I should skip my workout to prepare (yet again) for a presentation. Early on, I almost felt I needed permission—not from Craig, but from some unseen force telling me I hadn't earned it.

But when I began saying yes to myself—declaring, "I'm going to 7:00 a.m. yoga on Thursday," instead of waiting for permission—I felt the shift. Not just in my body, but in our entire household. At first, Craig might have felt the burden of morning responsibilities shifting to him. But soon, we both noticed the difference: I came home grounded, energized, and present. My attitude softened. My clarity sharpened. The ripple effect was undeniable. And soon, he *wanted* me to do it more often, realizing how much it fueled me.

The same happened with my morning coffee and reflection ritual. Instead of grabbing Starbucks on the way to work, I woke early to prepare my own wellness elixir. Craig, initially puzzled, noticed how this small act changed our mornings. I wasn't rushing out the door reactive, I was stepping into my day calm, clear, and aligned. Over time, he embraced the ritual too—not just for the health benefits, but for the energy it brought into our mornings and our family.

These small, intentional choices—prioritizing what nourishes me over what seems urgent—didn't just change me. They changed the energy of our home, our marriage, and how I showed up in my work. I realized that when I chose to fill myself up—not to escape, but to align—I became a better version of myself for everyone around me.

When you embody presence, you cultivate presence around you.

When you model a life that prioritizes alignment over approval, peace over pressure, and nourishment over neglect, you create permission slips for others to do the same.

When you show up whole, you invite wholeness in others. When you embody presence, you cultivate presence around you.

That's what modeling rituals in a culture of overdrive is really about. You don't need permission to take care of yourself. The well-being you cultivate doesn't stop with you—it radiates outward. It elevates your relationships, your family, your work, and your world.

Culture Isn't a Motto. It's a Mirror

Culture isn't declared, it's demonstrated. It's not found in mission statements but in micro-moments no one writes policies about, yet everyone feels.

Gallup's 2024 report reveals that the top reasons for disengagement at work aren't about pay or perks—they're about stress, lack of clarity, and disconnection from purpose. These point directly to leadership. Every leader—whether of a team, project, company, or family—sets the tone. Micro-cultures within teams shape the macro-culture of the entire organization.

You can't PowerPoint your way into belonging. But you can breathe it into the room.

I've seen the simplest rituals shift entire teams. A two-minute check-in: "How are you arriving today?" A brief "weather report" where each person shares their inner forecast. These aren't just exercises, they build psychological safety, the foundation of true engagement and contribution.

Now think about family. In the one you were raised in—or the one you're raising—is there an unspoken tension? Someone whose mood silently controls the room?

At our dinner table, we sometimes share "roses and thorns"—two moments of beauty and one challenge. Our parenting is far from perfect, but this is how we choose to model presence, transparency, and truth.

When you ritualize connection, you don't just shift culture, you restore humanity.

Ritualized Lives: The Secret Shared by the World's Most Impactful Leaders

You've now seen how living and leading with intention transforms not just your inner landscape but your outer impact. And the remarkable thing is you're not alone on this journey.

Some of the world's most impactful leaders—across industries, disciplines, and personal stories—have one thing in common: They've ritualized how they fit in what truly matters. They've learned to remove what no longer serves them, to honor their energy and focus, and to lead from a place of clarity and alignment.

This isn't reserved for a rare few. It's a conscious choice—one that you've begun to embody.

When you integrate the tools, rituals, and mindset shifts you've discovered in these pages, you step into a reserved but powerful lineage. You align yourself with leaders like

- Satya Nadella, CEO of Microsoft: Starts his day with poetry and reflection to cultivate empathy and clarity.
- Arianna Huffington, founder of Thrive Global: Prioritizes sleep, gratitude, and unplugging from technology.
- Marc Benioff, CEO of Salesforce: Regularly meditates and promotes mindfulness company-wide.
- Ray Dalio, founder of Bridgewater: Practices transcendental meditation and radical self-inquiry.
- Oprah Winfrey, chairwoman of OWN: Centers her life around gratitude, intention, and spiritual alignment.
- Jeff Bezos, founder of Amazon: Starts his mornings slowly, reflecting and preserving mental clarity.
- Reid Hoffman, co-founder of LinkedIn: Prioritizes daily reading, journaling, and deep reflection on failure and feedback.
- Stewart Butterfield, co-founder of Slack: Integrates long walks, journaling, and mindfulness into his daily rhythm, and builds reflection into company culture.

These leaders aren't successful because they hustle harder. They're successful because they've cultivated rituals of clarity, focus, and presence. They've started fitting in what matters most—just like you are learning to do.

And the most powerful growth is removing everything that never belonged to you in the first place.

So, as you continue this journey, remember: You're not only transforming yourself. You're joining a global circle of leaders who live intentionally, lead authentically, and model what's possible when you prioritize alignment over accumulation.

The future you're stepping into isn't a solo path. It's a collective evolution, and you're already a part of it.

You Are the Culture You Crave

By now, you've felt the shift—subtle, yet unmistakable. What began as private recalibration has become public presence. The rituals you once practiced for your own well-being have evolved into a quiet force, shaping not just your inner world, but the energy you bring into every room.

You've done more than adopt new habits. You've created a living architecture for how you lead, connect, and show up. You've dismantled outdated beliefs and reclaimed your time, energy, and focus—not as luxuries, but as your birthright.

Your rituals are touchstones—soulful anchors that nourish and sharpen your presence. Boundaries have become bold declarations of self-respect. Resilience is no longer about pushing harder, but moving with grace, intention, and trust in yourself.

These practices aren't strategies, they are the essence of the leader you've become. They grant you the capacity to stay grounded in chaos, navigate resistance with courage and compassion, and influence not through force, but through alignment.

This chapter marks a pivotal shift: where personal transformation becomes collective impact. Where your embodied leadership, presence, and coherence inspire others to step into their own.

The foundation is laid. The rituals are in place. The clarity is yours.

Now it's time to fully live this way of being—not as an exercise, but as an expression of who you've become.

CONCLUSION

The Life You Were Meant to Lead

Live your best life—it's your most important journey.
Oprah Winfrey

As you've come to understand, *I Can Fit That In* was never merely a mantra, nor about time. It was—and is—a mindset that is optimistic about fitting in life-giving rituals and knows when to cut things out of the schedule if they are life draining.

If you've reached this point, pause—not to ask *What's next?* but to feel *What's now*. The calm, steady hum of a life reclaimed. The subtle, almost imperceptible shift from proving to being. From exhaustion to embodiment. From chasing what depletes to choosing what nourishes.

This journey reminds me of the luna moth—the symbol you've seen on the cover of this book. Its significance now feels even more resonant. The luna moth spends the first part of its life as a caterpillar with an insatiable appetite, consuming as much as possible in a frantic bid for survival. It devours without rest, driven by instinct to accumulate, to grow, to become. But then, an extraordinary transformation unfolds. Emerging from its cocoon, the luna moth lives for just one week—a fleeting, delicate existence where it no longer eats, no longer chases, but simply exists. Its sole purpose is to reproduce, to perpetuate life, to be fully itself in the beautiful, brief window of life it's given as this stunning creature.

I see so much of my old self in the caterpillar—the relentless striving, the hunger for achievement, the constant devouring of time and energy in an attempt to feel worthy. But the luna moth's final chapter offers a profound reminder: Life is not about accumulation, but alignment. It's about emerging from the tunnel-vision cocoon of attaining and proving and stepping into a life that is intentional and true.

Like the luna moth, we are called not to consume endlessly, but to live fully in the fleeting moments we're given. To let go of the insatiable hunger for more, and instead honor what nourishes us. To recognize that our value is not in what we produce or achieve, but in the presence we bring, the connections we nurture, and the authenticity we embody.

That realization wasn't a dramatic epiphany—it was a quiet decision. A promise that if something didn't fuel my energy, my clarity, or my spirit, I was no longer available for it. That was the birth of *I Can Fit That In*.

A radical reframe of value. Not a productivity slogan. Not a lifehack. A declaration:

> **I Can Fit In** what fuels me, because I refuse to spend my life chasing what drains me.
>
> **I Can Fit In** my breath, my presence, my boundaries, because they are the architecture of my well-being.

I Can Fit In rituals that nourish, relationships that elevate, and choices that align with my truth.

And here's what I've learned, and what you, too, have discovered through these pages: When you begin to live deliberately, with presence and discernment, *everything changes*. Not overnight. Not in grand, sweeping gestures. But in the small, courageous decisions to stop proving and start living.

You've traveled this path.

In part 1, you started to reverse the numbness you got used to and challenged your outdated beliefs about self-worth, productivity, and success. You learned that reigniting the spark within can help you connect with the younger version of yourself that wasn't fazed by the structures you inherited as an adult.

In part 2, you embraced the power of ritual—not as a constraint, but as a container for energy, clarity, and intention. You rewired your rhythms, designed practices that nourished you, and discovered that rituals aren't something you *add* to life, they *become* life.

In part 3, you extended that inner alignment outward, infusing your leadership, relationships, and impact with authenticity and presence. You realized that your greatest influence isn't your words or strategies, it's the energy you bring into every room.

And now, here you are—not at an ending, but at the threshold of a life wholly, unapologetically your own.

This isn't a conclusion. It's an epilogue—a passage into the real story. The one where you no longer wait for a future when life feels full. You're living it. Right now.

You're no longer learning concepts and strategies or gaining knowledge; you possess skills, tools, practices, and wisdom.

You've cultivated the muscle of discernment—the ability to say no with clarity and yes with conviction. You've learned to protect your peace, to honor your energy, and to lead from within. And most importantly, you've remembered that you don't need fixing. Transformation is becoming yourself, and living so aligned with your truth that your very presence is a force of calm, clarity, and confidence.

How I Learned to Live This Way: Closing Reflection

As I shared at the beginning of this journey, I didn't set out seeking clarity or wisdom. I was simply chasing stability—a stable income, a stable reputation, a stable sense of worth. I was in my upper thirties, steeped in the belief that success meant proving, pushing, performing—being everything to everyone and leaving nothing undone. But the truth was that I was exhausted, fragmented, and silently desperate for permission to stop running.

The pivotal conversation with Craig that Friday night in 2017 wasn't just a random moment—it was a mirror. A reflection of how far I'd drifted from myself, how long I'd ignored the ache that whispered beneath the noise of my life. That night forced me to confront not just the weariness of an overextended schedule, but the deeper cost: the spiritual erosion, the disconnection from my own desires, the hollowing out of my joy.

Later, in Bali, surrounded by the stark simplicity of a world far removed from my own, the questions within me had been swirling and rose to the surface again: *What does this all mean? What's it all for?* I had just finished reading *The Untethered Soul* by Michael Singer, and every word in that book seemed to speak directly to my soul. I knew, on a visceral level, that I had a vast reservoir of inner work to do: to release old pain, to heal long-held emotional baggage, to move beyond the scripts and negativity that cluttered my mind. To become my own ally rather than my own adversary.

The first belief I dared to challenge was the one that had gripped me the tightest—the story we're all told: *Work hard, climb the ladder, earn your success, and one day, maybe at sixty-five, you'll finally get to live your life.* But I knew all too well how false that promise was. My father had been terminally ill at forty-five, gone by fifty-eight. He never got to ride into the sunset of retirement. He never got to experience the "someday" that so many of us are conditioned to wait for.

The lie unraveled itself in my mind, thread by thread: **This isn't the life we're meant for. This can't be the purpose of our precious, fleeting days.** I realized that waiting for retirement, waiting for permission to rest, waiting for external validation was a dangerous postponement of living. So I called it what it was: a myth, a trap, a script I could no longer subscribe to.

And once I saw it for what it was, I knew that new beliefs weren't going to emerge on their own. I had to plant them, water them, and nurture them like seeds. I had to think the thoughts that would serve my future self, even when the old ones still shouted for attention.

I didn't break free from these beliefs overnight. It took months of deliberate, steady inner work. Small yet profound shifts, layered one on top of the other. The people around me noticed the differences first. My family, friends, even strangers sensed the shift—the groundedness, the softer presence, the rising clarity. And slowly, I noticed it too. I was choosing differently. Choosing to read or journal or listen to a nourishing podcast instead of numbing out with social media. Choosing music over the relentless churn of news. Choosing to silence notifications, to be fully present with my kids instead of being physically there but mentally absent.

I learned to enter each day with intention— choosing what mattered and releasing what didn't.

I stopped collapsing into bed depleted and anxious. I stopped waking up with that tight, frantic feeling of being behind before the day had even begun. The burdensome anxiety about worst-case scenarios gave way to a muted trust that things could, in fact, turn out well. I stopped criticizing myself, stopped second-guessing every thought or interaction. I learned to enter each day with intention—choosing what mattered and releasing what didn't.

Personally, I became more patient, more connected, more alive in my own life. The resentment I'd quietly carried toward Craig began to dissolve—not because he changed, but because I did. I realized that resentment was my own to heal, not his to fix. I sat with it in stillness, asked myself the hard questions, journaled through the layers, visualized what a relationship free of resentment might feel like, and I saw the truth: My resentment wasn't about him. It was rooted in the belief that I was supposed to do it all, be everything to everyone, and that if I couldn't, I was failing.

This belief, so ingrained in the narrative of working women, was a lie I could no longer tolerate. The idea that we're meant to "balance" it all is a recipe for depletion and disappointment, leaving us feeling like lesser versions of ourselves. When I released this belief, I stopped waiting for appreciation and started offering it to myself. I began to receive the support I craved, because I modeled it for myself, not demanded it from others.

Morning by morning, ritual by ritual, I reclaimed my sanctuary. My living room became my solstice—a calm, cozy haven where I sipped my coffee elixir, read, journaled, and visualized the life I was creating. I built micro rituals throughout the day—breathing deeper into my belly, using the 4-7-8 method during stressful times, claiming moments for self-care even amidst busy workdays. These were not luxuries; they were life preservers.

Professionally, the transformation was equally profound. I stopped doing everything, stopped trying to control outcomes, and started listening—really listening. My decisions became clearer, my boundaries firmer, and my creativity sharper. I attracted dream clients not through hustle, but through presence. I reawakened my creativity, pouring it into writing and sharing my reflections publicly. And to my surprise, the world responded.

I was invited to speak—not once, but repeatedly. First at townhalls and small business events, then at Spotify for a sales team offsite titled "Do Good for Yourself, Do Good in the World." It felt like the universe, and my own soul, were conspiring to show me the path forward. Those early invitations revealed to me a deeper purpose—one I couldn't have imagined while stuck in my old way of transactional living.

Within a couple of years, I left corporate life to start my own business. I continued cultivating self-awareness, refining rituals, letting go of distractions and relationships that no longer aligned with who I was becoming. And with every level of clarity, new doors opened—opportunities, ideas, connections. The more I honored my alignment, the more life responded with ease and grace.

I realized that true transformation wasn't about time management or scheduling hacks, it was about shifting my internal state. About bringing a different energy into each moment. About cultivating the quiet confidence to live by design, not default. To nourish myself like my life depended on it. Because it did.

And so does yours.

If you're wondering how long it takes to create this shift, know this: It's already underway. It won't happen overnight, but it will happen through steady, intentional practice. And as you continue, the new way of being will feel as natural as breathing.

Your Power Is in the Return

You don't need to be perfect. You don't need to get it right every time. I certainly haven't. We're humans, not machines. There have been moments when I've slipped—late-night emails, mindless scrolling, default yeses to things that didn't align. But I've learned that slipping isn't regression. It's an invitation to pause, to breathe, to remember, and to begin again.

That's what rituals are for. They aren't constraints meant to box you in—they are anchors, gentle reminders that call you back to yourself. Each time you notice yourself slipping into old patterns—when life feels loud, when you feel stretched too thin—it's not a signal of failure. It's your next opportunity to return. You don't restart at ground zero, you pick up where you left off.

To come back to the practices you've built. To recall the clarity you've claimed. To step back into the presence and leadership you've embodied.

I can tell you from my own journey that power isn't proven by never falling off the track; it's in how quickly, gently, and courageously you get back on track.

The Journey Forward: You Can Fit That In

I Can Fit That In is a profound, soul-level choice.

You can fit in the breath. The walk. The honest conversation. The silent moment to check in with your heart. The weekly ritual that realigns you. The courage to say no. The audacity to say yes to something that lights you up.

You can fit in the life that's built on truth, not trend.

You can fit in the pause before the next big decision, the space to feel joy again, the moments that ground you in who you are becoming.

And you've already begun.

This isn't the finish line; it's an inflection point: a doorway into a life where every decision, every breath, every relationship is infused with intention. From here, you will still stretch. You will still be called to grow, to experience discomfort, to evolve. But now, you will stretch with intention, evolve with integrity, and lead not just from vision, but from embodiment.

You're no longer wondering if the life you want is possible. You're living it. One ritual, one choice, one clear, unwavering yes at a time.

When you embrace *I Can Fit That In* not just as a mindset, but as a way of being, you unlock a series of profound truths:

> **You are here to fill your life with what matters most.**
> **Your rituals are your architecture.**
> **Your presence is your influence.**
> **Your energy is your legacy.**

By embodying these principles, you align yourself with the world's most inspiring leaders—those who elevate not only themselves, but the people and the world around them.

And always, always remember:

You can fit that in.

Because you are ready to live fully, authentically, and intentionally as the person you were always meant to be.

This is your moment. The new default isn't busyness, depletion, and proving. It's vitality, presence, and discernment.

You're already on your way.

Keep listening.

Keep choosing.

Keep living—fully awake and aligned.

The world is waiting for the most radiant, authentic version of you. And the world will be a better place because of you.

APPENDIX

A Living Reminder:
You Can Fit That In

This page is your compass. Return to it when life gets noisy, when clarity feels distant, or when you're tempted to slip back into the rush. Let it bring you home.

I am ...
An intentional, grounded human being who creates with clarity and grace. I lead my life from the inside out, anchored in what matters. My presence is my power.

I value ...
Presence over performance. Progress over perfection. Truth over approval. Energy over ego. Wholeness over hustle. Depth over distraction. Purpose over pressure.

I release ...
The need to prove. The urge to please. The addiction to busyness. The belief that my worth is tied to output. The myth that more is always better.

I choose …
Rituals that renew me. Boundaries that protect me. Words that reflect me. Actions that align with me. A life that feels as good on the inside as it looks on the outside.

I Can Fit That In.
I can fit in the walk. The breath. The reset. The silence. The laughter. The stillness. The pause. The thing I keep putting off that brings me joy. The time to listen. The truth-telling moment. The space to just be.

Because what matters *can* fit in my life.

Because I now know how. My time, my energy, my peace are my mine to protect.

This isn't the end of my journey, it's the beginning of the one I was always meant to live.

Acknowledgements

To my parents—Your lives were marked by pain, struggle, and wounds no child should have to witness and no soul should have to carry alone. You both navigated more adversity than most ever will, and in doing so, you unknowingly handed me a map—not of where to go, but of what to rise from.

I know now that you did the best you could with what life gave you. And even when it wasn't enough, it still taught me more than you could have known: how to feel deeply, how to survive with grace, how to search for meaning beyond the material, and ultimately, how to choose differently.

Because of where I came from, I've dared to live in a way that defies logic and breaks convention. I've walked away from safety to follow the voice of my own spirit. I've made choices that society might judge and challenged the mainstream—paths that looked reckless, even irresponsible, from the outside. But they've been the most courageous, soul-aligned decisions of my life.

In witnessing your pain, I learned the value of peace. In absorbing your heartbreak, I learned the necessity of healing. In feeling what was never said, I learned to speak my truth. You showed me what it means to live with emptiness. And for that reason, I have devoted my life to fullness.

Thank you for giving me life, and through that life, the clarity to choose a new way forward: a way of wholeness, authenticity, and purpose. This book is part of that journey. And in some small way, part of your legacy too.

To my sons, Gramercy and Landen—I know this book asked something of you. It took me away at times, and I imagine it didn't always make sense why Mom needed quiet or space, or why I seemed so focused on something you couldn't quite see. But one day, you will. One day, you'll understand that this was more than "work"—this was my soul's mission. A legacy of love, truth, and purpose. And my hope is that watching me honor my own dreams plants the seed for you to pursue yours, unapologetically and wholeheartedly. You are my greatest teachers and my deepest inspiration. I love you to the sky times infinity times forever and ever.

To my clients—You brought me into your company with full faith that I would deliver not just excellence but something meaningful, real, and lasting. Thank you for trusting me; for welcoming me into your boardrooms, company events, and executive circles; and for giving me the immense privilege of guiding your teams, empowering your leaders, and helping your people return to the most powerful version of themselves.

Whether it was through a keynote on stage, a workshop in the office, a quiet moment of reflection at a retreat, or the sacred container of coaching—you allowed me to meet you where you were, and walk with you toward where you were meant to go. That trust is something I have never, and will never, take lightly.

To those who've shared my work and referred me to someone you care about—You've expanded my impact more than any marketing strategy ever could. You've trusted that when you introduce me to someone, I won't just show up, I'll pour my heart into the relationship. Because that's what this work is: human to human, leader to leader, and soul to soul.

This book is, in many ways, for the ones who care deeply and lead intentionally. And it's about doing business in a way that honors both the result *and* the relationship. Thank you for believing in me. And for allowing me to believe even more deeply in what's possible.

To my newsletter readers, podcast listeners, and LinkedIn community—You've witnessed my voice evolve. You've stayed with me as I've stepped more fully into my truth, and I see you too. Your messages, encouragement, and reflections have fueled me in quiet seasons when the road was long and unseen.

To Brooke Adams of Brooke & Mortar—From the very beginning, you've seen me. Not just the business or the brand, but the soul underneath it all. Your brilliance in design, integrity in every detail, and ability to translate my vision into something beautiful and alive could never be overstated and I am thankful for the gift you've been. Thank you for believing in what I was building long before the world could see it. You're not just a partner in creativity; you're part of the fabric of this mission.

To every person along my winding path who ever looked me in the eye and said, "You're meant for more"—You may not have known what that meant, and neither did I. But you planted a belief in me that became a compass. And over time, those words have revealed themselves to be both prophecy and invitation.

To the ones who doubted me—Who told me I'd never go to college. That I'd never make it in New York. That I was too much, too ambitious, or too idealistic. That I'd never find someone who could love all of me. Your words were meant to limit, but instead, they liberated. What you saw as rebellion was actually devotion—to truth, to vision, to possibility. Your doubt became my determination. I alchemized your projections into propulsion. I forgave, I released, and I rose. So, thank you. Thank you for underestimating me—it was fuel I didn't know I needed.

To Oprah—From the time I was a little girl, watching you through the static of our modest TV, you were more than a host—you were a beacon. A mirror of possibility. Your voice carried wisdom, warmth, and truth into homes like mine, where access was limited but dreams were limitless.

You spoke of self-worth, rising above circumstance, and listening to the whisper before it becomes a scream. Long before I had the language for healing or authenticity, I had you. You helped me believe that someone with a painful past and big dreams could carve a meaningful path.

Those hours spent watching you with my dad became a silent ritual—formative, sacred, and filled with hope. You gave both of us something precious: for me, a vision of what was possible; for him, perhaps a glimmer of gratitude he could still feel.

Thank you for leading with soul, speaking with intention, and showing us what it means to live on purpose. This book—and the life it reflects—owes something to the seeds you planted in me all those years ago.

And to every soul who has walked with me on this path—Whether through a single conversation, a passing connection, a lifelong friendship, or a shared moment of vulnerability—thank you. You've shaped me, softened me, and strengthened me. You've mirrored truths I wasn't ready to name and held space for dreams I was just beginning to imagine. This book is not simply a collection of insights. It's a tribute—to growth, to courage, to the sacred beauty of becoming. To what's possible when we stop performing and start listening to our intuition.

Bibliography

American Psychological Association.
2023 Work in America Survey: Workplace Health and Well-Being.
Washington, DC: American Psychological Association, 2023.
https://www.apa.org/pubs/reports/work-in-america/2023-workplace-health-well-being.

Brancato, Giuliana, Kathryne Van Hedger, Marc G. Berman, and Stephen C. Van Hedger. "Simulated Nature Walks Improve Psychological Well-Being Along a Natural to Urban Continuum." *Journal of Environmental Psychology* 81 (2022): 101779.
https://doi.org/10.1016/j.jenvp.2022.101779.

Brown, Brené. "Dare to Lead List of Values." *Brené Brown.* Accessed June 21, 2025.
https://brenebrown.com/resources/dare-to-lead-list-of-values/.

Brown, Brené. *Daring Greatly: How the Courage to Be Vulnerable Transforms the Way We Live, Love, Parent, and Lead.*
New York: Gotham Books, 2012.

Collins, Jim. "Books." *JimCollins.com.* Accessed June 21, 2025.
https://www.jimcollins.com/books.html.

De Witte, Melissa. "James Doty on the Neuroscience of Manifestation."
Stanford Report, May 10, 2024.
https://news.stanford.edu/stories/2024/05/james-doty-on-the-neuroscience-of-manifestation.

Dhingra, Naina, Jonathan Emmett, Andrew Samo, and Bill Schaninger. "Igniting Individual Purpose in Times of Crisis." *McKinsey Quarterly*, August 18, 2020. https://www.mckinsey.com/capabilities/people-and-organizational-performance/our-insights/igniting-individual-purpose-in-times-of-crisis.

Eurich, Tasha. "What Self-Awareness Really Is (and How to Cultivate It)." *Harvard Business Review*, January 4, 2018. https://hbr.org/2018/01/what-self-awareness-really-is-and-how-to-cultivate-it.

Fragale, Alison. "Alison Fragale | Professor | Keynote Speaker | Negotiation & Power Expert." *AlisonFragale.com*. Accessed June 21, 2025. https://www.alisonfragale.com/.

Goh, Joel, Jeffrey Pfeffer, and Stefanos A. Zenios. "The Relationship Between Workplace Stressors and Mortality and Health Costs in the United States." *Management Science* 62, no. 2 (March 13, 2016): 608–28. https://doi.org/10.1287/mnsc.2014.2115.

Killingsworth, Matthew A., and Daniel T. Gilbert. "A Wandering Mind Is an Unhappy Mind." *Science* 330, no. 6006 (November 12, 2010): 932–33.

LeFurgy, Jennifer, Ph.D. "Gallup Report Indicates Need for In-Person, Engaged Workplaces." *NAIOP Blog*, June 27, 2024. https://blog.naiop.org/2024/06/gallup-report-indicates-need-for-in-person-engaged-workplaces/.

Pink, Daniel H. *When: The Scientific Secrets of Perfect Timing*. New York: Riverhead Books, 2018.

Pressfield, Steven. *The War of Art: Break Through the Blocks and Win Your Inner Creative Battles*. New York: Warner Books, 2003.

Sadhguru (Jagadish Vasudev). *Inner Engineering: A Yogi's Guide to Joy*. New York: Spiegel & Grau, 2016. ISBN 9780812997798.2022 Journal of Environmental Psychology

Sood, Rishi. "What Is the Default Mode Network's Link to Mental Health?" *Amen Clinics*, June 11, 2024. https://www.amenclinics.com/blog/what-is-the-default-mode-networks-link-to-mental-health/.

Watkins, Michael D. "7 Ways to Weave Mindfulness into Your Workday." *Harvard Business Review*, July 16, 2024. https://hbr.org/2024/07/7-ways-to-weave-mindfulness-into-your-workday.

Winston, Diana, and Marvin Belzer. "Practicing Mindfulness Can Help to Relieve the Stresses of Difficult Times." *UCLA Health*, April 18, 2022. https://www.uclahealth.org/news/publication/practicing-mindfulness-can-help-relieve-stresses-difficult.

About Erin

Erin Coupe is the founder and CEO of Authentically EC, a coaching and speaking practice dedicated to helping professionals and organizations elevate leadership, align well-being, and enrich life—both personally and professionally.

Before launching her business in 2020, Erin spent over 17 years in the corporate world, holding executive positions at global firms including Goldman Sachs and CBRE. Her shift from Wall Street to transformational guide was sparked by a personal awakening—a journey from self-sabotage to self-leadership. She immersed herself in neuroscience, quantum mechanics, and spiritual study, blending these insights with real-world experience to create a uniquely grounded and expansive approach to growth.

Today, Erin is recognized as a thought leader in modern leadership, personal development, and self-transformation. Her clients include Fortune 1000 companies, global associations, universities, and professional sports organizations. Through speaking and keynotes, workshops, leadership coaching, and small group masterminds, Erin equips individuals and organizations with the human-centered skills essential for leading and living well.

Known for her ability to energize, empower, and deeply connect with her audiences, Erin helps professionals reclaim their time and focus and redefine success with a more mindful, sustainable approach to leadership. She is also the host of the popular podcast, *I Can Fit That In.*

Erin lives just north of Chicago with her husband and two boys. When she's not speaking, coaching, or creating, you'll find her writing, cooking something delicious (but never baking), or enjoying time in nature.

Share the Love

If this book moved you, sparked something within you, helped you reclaim even a moment of clarity, or transform what no longer works to what does, I'd be honored if you shared it.

Here's a few ideas on what to share:

- Post a photo or video of your favorite ritual in action.
- Snap a selfie with the book in your space: your desk, nightstand, travel bag, or your hands.
- Share your biggest shift or aha moment.
- Describe or quote for others what resonated most with you.

Tag me **@authenticallyEC** on Instagram and **@ErinCoupe** on LinkedIn so I can celebrate with you and continue growing this ripple of transformation together.

Because when you show up for yourself, you give others permission to do the same. Your story might just be the spark that helps someone else remember what they're truly here for.

Book Erin to Speak at Your Next Event

Whether it's a keynote to inspire transformation, a workshop to elevate leadership, or a session designed to empower and reconnect your team to what matters most, Erin brings clarity, authenticity, and actionable insights that leave a lasting impact.

From company offsites to large-scale conferences to women's network events and personalized leadership coaching, Erin customizes each experience to meet your audience where they are and guide them toward meaningful, sustainable change.

Let's create something powerful together.

Visit **erincoupe.com** to book Erin, or reach out directly at **hello@erincoupe.com** to start the conversation.

Stay in Touch with Me

📬 Join My Community and Newsletter

I'm known for thought leadership and high-value content that sparks clarity, catalyzes change, and adds a little more light to your world.

Sign up for free at **erincoupe.com/free-tools**.

✨ Apply to Join My Exclusive Leadership Cohorts

Immersive personal development experiences for leaders and executives ready to reconnect with what matters most and lead with more clarity, resilience and alignment—alongside a powerful, growth-minded community.

Learn more at **erincoupe.com/exclusive-community**.

🎧 Listen to the *I Can Fit That In* Podcast

Through intriguing, honest conversations with global thought leaders and high performers, you'll explore mindset shifts, pivotal moments, and the small changes that lead to lasting fulfillment.

New episodes are available wherever you get your podcasts or at **erincoupe.com/podcast**.

💬 Connect With Me on Social

Come say hi and connect with me:

LinkedIn: **linkedin.com/in/erin-coupe**
Instagram: **@authenticallyEC**
YouTube: **@erincoupe**

Learn more at **erincoupe.com**.

Notes

Notes

Notes

Notes

Notes

www.ingramcontent.com/pod-product-compliance
Lightning Source LLC
Chambersburg PA
CBHW050954050426
42337CB00051B/889